SMOKEHOUSE
HANDBOOK

SMOKE HOUSE

Handbook

Comprehensive Techniques &
Specialty Recipes for Smoking
Meat, Fish & Vegetables

JAKE LEVIN

Storey Publishing

The mission of Storey Publishing is to serve our customers by
publishing practical information that encourages
personal independence in harmony with the environment.

EDITED BY Carleen Madigan
ART DIRECTION AND BOOK DESIGN BY Jeff Stiefel
and Ash Austin
TEXT PRODUCTION BY Jennifer Jepson Smith
INDEXED BY Nancy D. Wood

COVER AND INTERIOR PHOTOGRAPHY BY © Keller +
Keller Photography
ADDITIONAL PHOTOGRAPHY BY Adam Morse/
Unsplash, 22; © beats_/stock.adobe.com, 18
bottom; © Big Green Egg, 77 left; © Brian
Overcast/Alamy Stock Photo, 5 bottom;
© De Agostini/G. Dagli Orti/Getty Images, 9;
Frieder Blickle, Export Organisation Südtirol,
der Handelskammer Bozen/Wikimedia
Commons, 8 top; © Gavin Kingcome
Photography/Getty Images, 108; © Goss
Images/Alamy Stock Photo, 72; Green Mountain
Grills, 77 right; © guy harrop/Alamy Stock
Photo, 73 bottom; Jake Levin, 7, 8 bottom, 79;
© Juhani Viitanen/Alamy Stock Photo, 6;
© kontrast-fotodesign/iStock.com, 18 top;
Mars Vilaubi, 29, 91, 116; © Matthiola/Alamy
Stock Photo, 4; © pastorscott/iStock.com, 11;
Provincial Archives of Alberta @ Flickr
Commons/Wikimedia Commons, 5 top;
© Stefano Carocci/iStock.com, 76; used by per-
mission of ultimatedrumsmokers.com, 73 top
left & right; © Zoonar GmbH/Alamy Stock
Photo, 103; © zlajaphoto/stock.adobe.com, 149
ILLUSTRATIONS BY © Michael Gellatly

TEXT © 2019 by Jake Levin

The information in this book is true and complete to the best of our knowledge. All recommen-
dations are made without guarantee on the part
of the author or Storey Publishing. The author and
publisher disclaim any liability in connection with
the use of this information.

Storey books are available at special discounts
when purchased in bulk for premiums and sales
promotions as well as for fund-raising or educa-
tional use. Special editions or book excerpts can
also be created to specification. For details,
please call 800-827-8673, or send an email to
sales@storey.com.

Storey Publishing
210 MASS MoCA Way
North Adams, MA 01247
storey.com

Printed in the United States by Versa Press
10 9 8 7 6 5 4 3 2 1

LIBRARY OF CONGRESS CATALOGING-IN-
PUBLICATION DATA

Names: Levin, Jake, author.
Title: Smokehouse handbook : comprehensive
    techniques & specialty recipes for smoking
    meat, fish & vegetables / by Jake Levin.
Description: North Adams, MA : Storey Publishing,
    [2019] | Includes bibliographical references
    and index. | Identifiers: LCCN 2019003122
    (print) | LCCN 2019003989 (ebook)
    | ISBN 9781635860122 (ebook)
    | ISBN 9781635860115 (hardcover : alk. paper)
Subjects: LCSH: Smoked foods. | Cooking
    (Smoked foods) | Cooking (Meat)
    | LCGFT: Cookbooks.
Classification: LCC TX835 (ebook)
    | LCC TX835 .L48 2019 (print)
    | DDC 641.6/16—dc23
LC record available at https://lccn.loc
    .gov/2019003122

Dedicated to my two brothers,
Will and Sam, and my wife, Silka.

TO WILL, for your willingness to try whatever
I cook and for your craftsmanship and
creativity as a builder. Without you there would
be no smokehouse and no book.

———————————————

TO SAM, for being my biggest fan as a
food writer and for your insightful edits
and suggestions for this book.

———————————————

TO SILKA, for always being there to support me
and for pretending to not mind that I am
usually covered in animal fat and soot and
always smell like smoke.

CONTENTS

SMOKE-FILLED BEGINNINGS

This book starts and ends in my backyard, with my wife, my two brothers, and me sitting around a fire, cooking dinner. In between, we will travel around the globe; touch on the history of *Homo sapiens*; talk about chemistry, biology, and physics; describe simple building techniques; and breathe in a lot of smoke. But, in the end, this book is about being in your backyard with your loved ones, eating delicious food you've smoked in a smoker you built.

I can't say exactly how I came to be so interested in smoking meats. Ever since I was a child, I have always loved meat — especially smoked and cured meats. The father of my best friend from childhood was Hungarian, and whenever there was an important holiday or gathering at their house, there would always be links of dark red, smoky, dry-cured sausages served. I couldn't resist those coin-sized medallions made of pork, paprika, and garlic, glistening with studs of white fat. Every movement I made through my friend's house involved a pass by the platter of sausage so I could surreptitiously pocket another small fistful of this delicacy. I will never forget the flavor and aroma of those sausages.

It wasn't until I was in my early twenties and living in Brooklyn that I first started to experiment with smoking meat myself. I was becoming increasingly bold in my at-home culinary experiments; in hindsight, this was when I began to realize I wanted to pursue a career in food. One day I decided to buy a stove-top smoker so I could start to try smoking myself. You can imagine how thrilled my roommates were when they came home to find our railroad apartment filled with cherry smoke and a partially raw whole chicken for dinner. But I didn't let that stop me. I continued to play, and I grew more ambitious.

The next year my girlfriend (now wife) and I decided to throw a Christmakkah party (now an annual event), and I insisted on brining and smoking a Christmas ham in our apartment. My stove-top smoker was too small for a ham, so I decided to turn our oven into a smoker. I turned the oven to 250°F (120°C) and placed a baking dish of sawdust on the bottom of the oven, which I kept smoldering with the assistance of a small propane blowtorch. For weeks after, our whole apartment smelled of applewood smoke.

Luckily for my wife (and our neighbors), I decided I wanted to work with meat professionally, and we moved to the Berkshires, in rural western Massachusetts, where I had grown up. My wife no longer had to worry that we would be kicked out of our apartment, and our neighbors were no longer subjected to the odd aromas emanating from our tiny kitchen. Moving to the country and becoming a professional butcher were major developments in my relationship to smoking meat.

I INSISTED ON BRINING AND SMOKING A CHRISTMAS HAM IN OUR APARTMENT. MY STOVE-TOP SMOKER WAS TOO SMALL FOR A HAM, SO I DECIDED TO TURN OUR OVEN INTO A SMOKER.

In my training as a whole-animal butcher, I gained a deeper understanding of meat and the various processes applied to meat production. I now understand much more about muscle structure and development, the biochemical changes that occur when a cure is applied to meat, the way fat behaves, and the effect different temperatures and levels of humidity can have on meat. Working in a butcher shop also meant I had access to equipment like a large electric smoker that I would never have in my home. My colleagues and I experimented a lot — we made smoked corned tongues, face bacon, smoked mutton leg (a.k.a. "shamb"), all kinds of smoked sausages, smoked rillettes, and smoked salt.

I was in nirvana: I had a group of meat-nerd colleagues, and I had a house with a backyard, where I could get as smoky and messy as I wanted. As soon as we moved into our house, I started designing my outdoor kitchen. I am very fortunate that my brother Will, who is a builder, loves smoked meats as much as I do. Together we designed a smokehouse, which he built (with some assistance from me). Our smokehouse, which we named Frazier (after the great boxer, Smokin' Joe Frazier, and our grandfather's farmhand, Willie Frazier, with whom we worked closely growing up), took a lot of experimenting and tinkering with to get to work just right; see page 168 for details on its design. Today, it is my happy spot and the workhorse of most of our family holidays. From early spring to early winter we are outside cooking, smoking, and experimenting.

Like any fanatic, I'm never fully satiated when it comes to the craft of smoking meat. Part of my love for smoking meats is all of the equipment that accompanies it. And so I continue to amass various smoking apparatuses and toys. Along with Frazier, I still have that first stove-top smoker, a large grill table, a Weber kettle grill, an upright barrel smoker, a donabe (a Japanese ceramic vessel used for cooking rice and smoking foods), and an electric smoker oven. I constantly experiment with different techniques, fuels for smoke, and smoking structures. I continue to find an indescribable joy and satisfaction in smoking meat and enjoying the results it provides.

I wanted to write this book because I want everyone to feel that same joy and satisfaction — and I want people to be able to find that joy and satisfaction a little more easily than I did. My smoked meat–filled journey has been beset by failed experiments; the most frustrating part was the lack of solid information on building a backyard smokehouse. Because there were so few resources to guide us, building Frazier was a long process with lots of missteps and rebuilding, correcting, and testing.

What I wished I'd had as I was learning, testing, and building was a book that would explain the basics of hot and cold smoking, as well as the process of smoking meat and the various fuels for generating smoke, designs for building smoking apparatuses and how to use them, and foundational recipes that I could experiment with and build upon. I hope that this book will provide you with all of that, and more.

PART 1

THE
BASICS

To be successful at smoking meat, you must consider the three main elements: the meat itself, the temperature at which you smoke the meat, and the source of the smoke. These elements can be brought together in different ways to create myriad delicious smoked products. It's important to consider the structure of the meat itself: Is it fatty or lean? Tough or tender? Also think about what kind of cure you'll be applying, whether it's a rub, a brine, or a full cure. Another decision is whether to hot smoke — fully cooking the meat — or cold smoke, which preserves and cures the meat. The smoke can come from sawdust, woodchips, or split logs — or from nonwood sources like straw or tea.

Once you have a firm grasp of these three elements, as well as the way in which they interplay, you'll have the knowledge you need to experiment freely and produce delicious smoked products in your own backyard.

❶

WHY WE SMOKE

- -

Before we go further, we should probably establish what smoking is. Smoking, at its most basic, is a form of preserving meat by exposing it to smoke from burning plant material (usually wood) over a period of time (anywhere from a couple of hours to a couple of weeks).

- -

Exposure to smoke helps to preserve meat in two ways. First, it helps to draw out the moisture. Second, smoke imparts various chemical compounds onto the surface of the meat, which kill or inhibit the growth of microbes and slow down the oxidization of the fat. It also happens to add a delectable flavor to the meat. The combination of its preservative effect on meat and its flavor enhancement made smoking so popular a process that it has withstood the advent of refrigeration. Today smoked foods are often considered a delicacy and are an ingrained part of the cultural history of many regions of the world. But how did we get to this place?

FROM THE CAVE TO THE BARBECUE

Envision a group of nomadic people. They have just completed a successful deer hunt and butchered the carcass, and they are getting ready to cook some of their favorite cuts. They're sitting around a fire inside a small shelter. In celebration of this successful hunt, they're cooking the back strap over the fire. There is more meat than they could consume in one meal, so they have salted and hung the other cuts of meat to dry from the top of the shelter. Some of that venison hangs over the fire, near the vent where the smoke from the fire escapes.

A couple of days pass, and they go to cut down and eat one of the pieces of venison that had been hanging near that vent. They notice that while the venison that wasn't hanging near the vent is starting to go rancid and is covered in flies, the venison *near* the vent appears to be still good to eat. They might notice that the texture and color of that venison is different. It has dried out evenly and is firm to the touch instead of being tacky and soft. The color of the flesh retains a redness instead of becoming a grayish brown. They bite into it and notice the flavor is different; it's better than it usually tastes after hanging for a few days. The venison hasn't turned at all, the fat isn't rancid, the meat doesn't taste rotten — it is smoky and delicious!

Although the nomads probably didn't have a complete understanding of why this meat was lasting longer than usual or why it tasted so mouthwateringly good, they did know they had stumbled upon something great. This was the beginning of smoking food, a process that has since become an indispensable part of human life and culture.

The process of smoking meats is utilized throughout the world, adapted to the culture and environmental conditions of each place. One of the things I love about smoking is that, for the most part, very little about the process and techniques has changed over time. Wherever you are in the world, you can find people smoking foods the same way their great-grandparents did — often using the same smokehouse their great-grandparents used. It's a wonderful example of how food becomes a representation of culture and environment.

Native Americans and people of the First Nations traditionally smoked venison, bison, and fish by cutting the meat into thin strips and hanging them from the top of their living structures or similar wooden structures to catch the smoke from the hearth as it vented out.

FIRST NATIONS JERKY AND EARLY BARBECUE

The Cree of the First Nations in Canada and the American Plains smoked meats up until the bison were nearly exterminated by white settlers. They would hang thin strips of bison from the top of their tepees and wigwams, or build miniature versions of those structures, catching the smoke as it rose from the hearth. The result was a smoky jerky that was easy to pack and could last for a long time. This was important, as the Cree were nomadic and followed the herds. Being able to preserve meat in a transportable form — especially from animals as large as bison, which yielded a large amount of meat — was indispensable for their way of life. This First Nations food staple has now become one of the most

Smoking meat was a practical way to preserve meat harvested from the hunt. This Cree woman is smoking meat in northern Saskatchewan.

Pit roasting whole animals, such as goats, wrapped in organic material like banana leaves is a centuries-old tradition in Central America. The wrapped meat is placed directly on a deep bed of hot coals in an earthen pit, covered, and left to slowly cook for hours.

common snacks of America, available at any gas station, convenience store, grocery store, or butcher shop across the country. Similarly, the tribes of the Pacific Northwest would smoke much of the salmon they caught during the summer and fall months, ensuring that they had food to take them through the cold and often hard winter season.

Farther south, in Mexico and Central America, a very different technique, called pit roasting, was used to cook meat. This process of cooking is part of the origin story of another staple of modern American cuisine — barbecue. Pit roasting is one of my favorite techniques, partly because it's still practiced today in its simplest form, and it results in unrivaled flavor and texture. One of the first times I experienced it was in Oaxaca. My brother was building a house for some friends there, and when it was complete, they celebrated by pit roasting a whole goat. When the goat was finally unearthed, the meat was falling off the bones and infused with a sweet, smoky scent from the maguey (the type of agave plant that mezcal is made from) the goat had been wrapped in. The meat had a wonderful silky quality. The gaminess of the goat was mellowed out by floral and grassy smokiness from the maguey. We ate the goat with some handmade wheat tortillas, a spicy salsa made from dried chiles, and mezcal.

The particulars of pit roasting — including the cut and type of meat and the material it's wrapped in — vary throughout Mexico and Central America, but the principle technique remains the same. Mexicans and Central Americans dig pits in which they build a deep bed of charcoal. Then they wrap a whole animal (or large portion, like a steer's head) in big leaves, usually banana, maguey, or corn husks. The meat is laid on the hot bed of coals and then covered and buried. It is left for hours, even overnight, and then it is uncovered, unwrapped, and eaten. This technique yields the most succulent meat with an amazing smoky aroma imparted by the burning coals and the leaves wrapped around the meat.

SMOKED FISH IN SCANDINAVIA AND WEST AFRICA

Across the Atlantic, various forms of salted and smoked fish — whether it's cod, flounder, salmon, herring, or mackerel — are an important part of the Scandinavian and British diets, as well as their cultural identities. When my wife and I went to visit her family on Faro, the easternmost island in Sweden, I kept seeing signs next to little white stone huts that announced *rokt flundra*. When I asked our hosts what this meant, they stopped and picked some up for us to try. *Rokt flundra* are smoked flounder fillets, a staple of the diet there. I quickly fell in love with them! The flesh was delicate and flaky, imbued with a light smoky flavor that made it taste the way a fire on the beach smells — briny and heady.

You will see similar small stone huts dotting the coasts of Scandinavia and Great Britain. The cold northern waters produce fatty fish, which have historically been an important part

In northern Europe, and especially Scandinavia, oily fish like salmon and mackerel are smoked over beech and oak in distinctive-looking white smokehouses along the shore.

of the diet, especially during the harsh winters. Traditional fishing patterns were based on the time of year when various species were running (swimming through those particular waters) and when they were spawning (breeding). Whatever type of fish the locals caught would spoil quickly, though, if it wasn't preserved; salting and smoking helped make the catch last. Inside those small stone shelters, the fish were (and still are, in many places) cleaned, salted, and then hung to smoke over small fires built on the shelter floor.

As in Scandinavia, fish is one of the staples of West African cuisine and there are many different methods for preserving it, including salting, air-drying, and cold smoking. Along the coast of Senegal and Ghana, the method of preserving fish that scents the air is traditional hot smoking. In long trenches, similar to the pits you see in the American South, fish are butterflied and set to smoke over millet grass (millet is one of the most common grains in the region) and then salted and fermented (a reversal of the process we use in North America). The smoked and salted fish is then used to flavor dishes. The smoky, briny scent of this process is inseparable from the experience of traveling the West African coast.

Throughout coastal West Africa, fish are salted and smoked over shallow pits of smoldering millet grass.

FROM SPECK TO CHAR SIU

Pork has been an indispensable part of European diet and culture for thousands of years — the first evidence of domesticated pork dates back to at least 5000 BCE. Traditionally pigs were slaughtered and processed in the fall. After farmers harvested the last of the vegetables, fruits, nuts, and grains, they would run their pigs through the fields and orchards to eat up what was left; the different crops they ate imparted different flavors in the meat. Once the weather was cool enough that the hot sun wouldn't spoil the meat, families would gather together to process their hogs. The pork harvested had to last until the following fall, so many of the cuts were salted and often smoked.

Depending on where you are in Europe, you'll find various versions of cured and smoked pig legs. One of my favorites comes from the southern part of the Alpine region, along the border of Italy and Switzerland. Here, whole pork legs are first cured in salt, juniper berries, rosemary, and bay leaves (all products that grow in the region) and then hung to smoke over juniper wood to produce speck. This fatty, salty, smoky, aromatic meat is eaten throughout the year with bread, cheese, and wine. (See the recipe on page 150.) On the northern edge of the Alps is another notable and probably more recognizable pork product — the Black Forest ham. This Bavarian delicacy is now a standard deli meat. The distinct flavor and color of the ham comes from the fact that it is smoked over fir and juniper.

Throughout China and Southeast Asia, you will find examples of pork infused with smoky flavor. In China, char siu (literally, "fork roasted") is a great example. Pork is slowly roasted over a wood fire and then lacquered with a sweet and salty sauce made with honey, soy sauce, and the Chinese five spices. In Southeast Asia, you can find racks of pork ribs cooking over smoldering wood, being slathered with a combination of herbs, spices, palm sugar, and fish sauce. One of my favorite smoking traditions (and favorite cuisines) comes from the Sichuan province. There, they let a whole duck or duck breasts marinate overnight in a cure of saltpeter, Sichuan pepper, and rice wine and then smoke it over a mixture of rice and tea (see recipe on page 109).

These techniques have existed across the world for a thousand years and are still being employed, largely unchanged, today. The only thing that has really changed is the necessity of preserving meat. We no longer smoke meats out of a need to preserve them, but out of a love for the effect that prolonged exposure to smoke has on them.

Throughout Southeast Asia, especially in the famed night markets, you will find metal grills covered in racks of pork ribs, thin slices of pork shoulder, whole fish, and pieces of chicken and duck slathered in chiles, various spices, palm sugar, and fish sauce and being slowly cooked over coals billowing smoke.

In the Alpine borderland between Germanic Switzerland, Austria, and Italy, you will find speck — pork shoulder cured with traditional spices like juniper berry, bay leaves, and rosemary, then smoked over juniper wood.

Jacques LeMoyne, a French illustrator, documented what he found on his visit to modern-day Florida in the mid-1500s. In this image, he recorded the traditional cooking technique called *barabicu*, in which fish and other meats were cooked on a set of thin sticks resting on wood posts over a fire.

THE ORIGINS OF AMERICAN BARBECUE

The advent of refrigeration has meant that smoking meats to preserve them is no longer a necessity. Luckily, this hasn't resulted in a decline in the craft of smoking meats. People continue to crave the unique flavor created when meat, salt, and smoke are combined. Today, smoked meats are an expression of place, culture, and history. What is China without its char siu? What is Poland without smoky kielbasa? What is Senegal without smoked fish?

One of the best examples of smoked meat as an embodiment of the melding of traditions, location, and heritage is American barbecue. The word "barbecue" is most likely derived from the word *barabicu* from the Arawak people of the Caribbean. *Barabicu* is translated as "a framework of sticks set upon posts," which is the structure on which the Arawak cooked meat. Essentially, the grill was also the fuel. This structure would have allowed for the meat to cook slowly as it was infused with smoke. *Barabicu* is also what gave us the word *barbacoa* — the method of cooking meats wrapped in leaves in a buried pit.

Modern American barbecue is the result of the mixing of Caribbean, Mesoamerican, Spanish, and African cooking styles in colonial America.

There has been a long tradition of smoking pork in Spain, mostly in the form of sausages. When the Spanish came to the Americas, not only did they bring this cooking style, but they also brought pigs and cows to establish European livestock as a food source, so they could continue their food culture in this foreign land. When they arrived, they encountered the cooking styles of the native Caribbean people and Native Americans.

In Mexico, the Spanish conquistadors learned the tradition of burying whole animals wrapped in maguey leaves, corn husks, or banana leaves in pits in the ground to slowly cook. This imparted a smoky toasted flavor to the meat and allowed the meat to cook slowly, resulting in an unctuous, silky texture. In Haiti, the Spaniards observed a method that involved cooking meat over a framework of slowly burning sticks, infusing a smoky flavor and allowing a gentle roasting of the meat. With the slave trade from West Africa, the classic accompaniments for barbecue, including slow-cooked hardy greens and roasted yams, were introduced to American Southern cuisine. Out of this (violent and forceful) mixing of cultures was born one of the great American food traditions.

AMERICAN BARBECUE TODAY

Today barbecue can be divided into several distinct styles: Carolina, Memphis, Kansas, and Texas. You can find pit masters in these regions who claim a barbecue lineage that goes back five generations. Each style is distinct, focusing on different cuts, animals, and smoke sources. Carolina barbecue is centered on whole hogs smoked over hardwoods like oak and maple. This is an area that was densely wooded, where the pigs the Spaniards brought over thrived. In Texas barbecue, it's all about beef smoked over hickory, mesquite, pecan, and peach wood.

Texas is a land of soft rolling hills and flat plains with shrubs and fruit trees, where the steers the Spaniards imported prospered. As you go from east (Carolinas) to west (Texas), you can see these styles blend, with more beef being used as you go farther west. Each style has its apostles and disciples. Many people (myself included) design trips just around eating barbecue in these regions. Heated debates are waged over which region's barbecue is best. Today we have internationally famous barbecue joints like Franklin Barbecue in Austin, Texas, and Wilber's Barbecue in Goldsboro, North Carolina, where people will wait in line for hours just for a taste of their smoky, meaty goodness.

In this day and age, one doesn't need to fly to Leadville to taste excellent authentic Texas smoked meats. On the tiny (but admittedly well-populated) island of Manhattan, one has access to northern European–style smoked fish, Texas barbecue brisket, Chinese char siu, Hungarian dried sausage, Ashkenazi Jewish pastrami, and much, much more. Each style of smoking still has its rich story to tell, and new styles continue to emerge, expressing the changes in modern culture. And while today there is an aura of luxury and mystique behind excellent smoked meats, it's important to remember their very humble and plain roots. It wasn't that long ago that most Americans had a smoker in their backyard.

Today, barbecue enthusiasts can still find different barbecue techniques and styles in various regions of the country. In Central and Southern California, pit masters often cook over actual open pits filled with slow-burning hardwood like oak. Because it's cattle country, most of the region's barbecue features beef.

2

CHOOSING A CUT TO SMOKE

- -

Although you don't need to be a trained butcher or chef to master the art of smoking meats, basic knowledge of meat is important for successful smoking.

- -

Understanding the structure of the cut of meat you're planning to smoke will help you make important decisions for the smoking process. Knowing how tough the meat is likely to be and how much fat is in it will help you determine how long to smoke it, what temperature to smoke it at, and what kind of cure to use. Understanding the fundamentals of meat ultimately allows you to experiment with more confidence and create your own delicious smoked products. The recipes and techniques in this book will provide you with a good framework to start from. After mastering the basics, you'll be able branch out on your own.

DISSECTING MEAT

Visualize a pork chop. In your mind, it probably has two or three components: muscle, fat, and maybe bone. The majority of the chop is made up of reddish-pink muscle. Then there is the yellowish-white fat, most of which encircles the muscle (this is called the *intermuscular* fat). You may also see some spiderwebbing of fat throughout the muscle itself, or what we call marbling (the *intramuscular* fat). You may notice some silvery-white material near where the bone meets the muscle. This is the connective tissue. And, possibly, there is a bone attached to the muscle. (Though for our purposes, we can ignore the bone.) These three kinds of tissues are made up of different amounts of water, protein, and fat.

Muscle cells make up long fibers that cause movement when they contract and relax. Surrounding the long muscle fibers is the connective tissue, which binds the muscle fibers together and to the bones that those fibers move. Third, but certainly not least, are the fat cells; these store the lipids that act as the fuel for the muscle fibers. The various qualities of the meat — texture, color, and flavor — are, to a large extent, governed by the configuration and proportion of the muscle fibers, connective tissue, and fat tissue.

As a side note, although the term "meat" can refer to any animal tissues that can be eaten, in the United States we tend to distinguish between muscle tissue whose function is to move some part of the animal and organ meat, such as the liver and kidneys. In this book, we'll use the term "meat" to refer to muscle tissue, since that is what most people smoke.

WHAT MAKES MEAT TENDER OR TOUGH

Depending on the actions the muscle controls in the animal (running, breathing, or eating, for example), the muscle will have different structures (called "crosslinks") that affect the color, texture (how tender or tough), and flavor of the resulting meat. The tenderness or toughness of a piece of meat is directly related to how heavily a muscle is worked: the more a muscle works, the more connective tissue is developed in the muscle, and the more flavor that muscle will have.

How do you know which muscles are heavily worked and which aren't? It's more straightforward than you might assume. If you'd like more information than the following overview provides, you'd do well to find a good and knowledgeable butcher who can help guide you through your options and explain to you what will work best for your needs.

The tenderloin (at left) is a tender, mild-tasting cut that comes from a relatively inactive muscle. The shoulder (at right) is tough but flavorful, a very active muscle webbed with intramuscular fat and connective tissue.

IDENTIFYING CUTS OF MEAT FOR SMOKING

Imagine a farm animal's life. It spends its days walking around a pasture lowering and lifting its head to forage around, getting up and lying down, and running around to play with the other farm animals. With this image in mind, you can start to figure out where the cuts with more connective tissue might be, and where the more tender cuts might be. But let's go through it together.

HEAD, NECK, AND SHOULDER: TOUGH BUT FLAVORFUL

The head and neck. These are some of the most worked muscles in the body, as most animals spend their days lifting and lowering their head looking for good forage to eat and using their cheek muscles to chew tough grasses, tubers, and roots. Because of this, head and neck muscles provide some of the best meat on the animal. Cooking them slowly, over a long period of time, at a low temperature, will transform the bundles of connective tissue and muscle into something with unbelievably delicious texture and flavor. That's why I always ask for meat from the jowl and neck when I'm at a pig roast.

The shoulder. Moving down the animal, you will find the shoulder. In beef, this part of the animal is referred to as the chuck; it includes the brisket, short ribs, and foreshank. In lambs, goats, and pigs it is simply called the shoulder. In pork, the shoulder is further divided into the upper shoulder (also called the "butt") and the lower shoulder (also called the picnic ham). The group of muscles that make up the shoulder do a lot of work: they support the lifting and lowering of the head and neck, bear the weight of the animal when it stands, and control the movement of the forelegs as the animal moves around. With all of this action, the various muscles here develop a large amount of connective tissue.

FROM FACE BACON TO PORK SHOULDER

It takes some research to find smoking recipes that call for using the head and neck, but they are out there. In Mexico and Central America, the head is traditionally slow-roasted in a pit to make *barbacoa.* Pit roasting a steer's head is a cowboy classic; another great preparation for head meat is "face bacon." For this, you can ask your butcher for a deboned pig's head and then treat it just like you would a belly for bacon (see the recipe on page 123).

The shoulder is a versatile cut with a ton of flavor and is relatively affordable. You can use shoulder to make sausage, speck, and cottage bacon, but nothing beats Carolina-style smoked pulled pork.

The shoulder gives us two of the most famous (and delicious) cuts for American barbecue: pork shoulder and beef brisket (see the recipes on pages 112 and 115). This is also where you would get beef short ribs or pork country ribs, both of which are fantastic hot-smoked. The shoulder is also the ideal cut for making sausage because it has great flavor and the right ratio of lean muscle to fat — most shoulders are about 70 percent lean muscle and 30 percent fat. The act of grinding the meat mitigates the effect of the dense connective tissue. The shoulder also gives us some of my favorite dry-cured products like speck (see the recipe on page 150). Or you can turn the foreshanks of the pig into ham hocks (see the recipe on page 99).

THE "MONEY MEAT": RIBS, LOIN, AND TENDERLOIN

Next up is the middle section, which is worth thinking about in terms of the upper section and lower section. The upper section — what we butchers refer to as the "money meat," because it contains the cuts that fetch the highest price — includes rib cuts, loin cuts, and the tenderloin. These muscles are the least active and therefore the most tender. The cuts include New York strip steaks and rib eyes for beef, lamb loin chops and lamb rib chops, and pork chops and tenderloin (aptly named because it's the most tender muscle in the body; a so-called "inactive" muscle, its main purpose is to protect the animal's vital organs).

A QUICK SMOKE ON THE GRILL

I don't generally smoke the money meat, although you can. More often, I just grill these cuts quickly over high heat and eat them on the rare side (including pork). That said, a smoked pork chop is fantastic, and quick to make. When I do smoke these cuts, it's generally on the grill. For instance, I might throw some woodchips over the fire to add some smoke for the final few minutes of grilling. In Canada, it's common

Tender cuts such as a porterhouse steak are relatively inactive and thus more tender. Give it a quick smoke by adding some sawdust or woodchips to the charcoal as you grill it.

to add some evergreen cuttings to the coals in the grill when grilling steaks, imparting a slightly bitter flavor. And speaking of Canadians, the loin is the cut that Canadian bacon comes from. Canadian bacon is simply a boneless pork loin brined and smoked, just like ham (see page 97). If you remove the bones from the loin you end up with baby back ribs, which are fantastic smoked. I prefer to leave the bone on the loin for pork chops and work with spare ribs. Leaving the bone on the pork chop results in meat with better flavor; plus, it's more fun to eat.

THE BELLY AND RIBS

Below the loin section is what's referred to as the belly in pork, the flank in beef, and the breast in lamb and goat. You might think these muscles are fairly inactive, but that's not totally true — there are few things as important to the life of an animal as breathing. As the animal breathes, all day every day, these muscles expand and contract. It is this expansion and contraction that accounts for the accordion-like texture of the beef cuts from this section: skirt steak and flank steak. This section is also where most of the ribs are cut from.

THE REAL PRIZE: BACON AND RIBS

In pork, the belly is the source of one of the most famous and prized smoked products in the world: bacon. Bacon is the whole belly cured and smoked (see page 123). Thanks in part to one of my mentors, the butcher Bryan Mayer, making bacon from this cut in other animals like lamb has become popular. My friends at Grow and Behold (an organic kosher meat delivery service based in New York City) have had huge success making beef bacon. This is a great way to use a cut that is normally just ground up. Another great cut for smoking from this section is the ribs. Ribs are my personal favorite, as much because of the fun of eating them as for any other reason. Any of these cuts can be hot-smoked for a medium amount of time (see page 111); they don't have the same amount of connective tissue as the shoulder, so they don't need a long smoke to break down that tissue.

THE HIND LEG

Now we arrive at the back end of the animal, which by no means should be thought of as the least desirable. In beef, this section is referred to as the round; in lamb and goat, the leg; and in pork, the ham. This section gets a lot of use, though it is not as active as the shoulder. While the shoulder is affected by the use of the neck and head, the hindquarter is merely responsible for the motion of the legs. So, although this section has more connective tissue than the middle section does, it doesn't have nearly as much as the shoulder, neck, and head.

The belly/rib section of the animal offers us some of the best cuts for smoking, such as bacon and ribs.

ALL ABOUT THE HAM

In beef, lamb, and goat there are not many cuts from this primal that are traditionally smoked. In beef, there is one cut that is sometimes smoked on the West Coast: the tri-tip. It's such a micro-regional cut that it's sometimes even called the Santa Maria tri-tip, referring to the town in California where it was first popularized. This is a cut you could smoke right on your grill, bringing it to a nice medium-rare.

When it comes to pork, the hindquarter provides one of the most important cuts for smoking: the mighty ham! Hams can be brined and hot smoked or dry cured and cold smoked. Throughout China, Europe, and North America, you will find all kinds of hams, although central and eastern Europe probably has the most variation. I tend to make either a traditional holiday ham, which I brine and hot smoke for a few hours, or a country ham, which I dry cure, cold smoke for a few days, and then hang for at least nine months (see page 151).

The hind leg can be smoked to produce any number of delicious products, including *jamón iberico* (top) and ham hocks (bottom).

FOWL AND FISH

Believe it or not, the general rules for thinking about the different cuts of poultry parallel those for four-legged animals, and the same logic applies in terms of muscle use, tenderness, and flavor. The basic cuts of poultry are wings, breast, and legs (made up of thigh and drumstick). Sometimes when you buy a chicken or turkey the neck is included. Just as with pork, the meat of smoked poultry neck is unrivaled in flavor. On Thanksgiving, I save the neck of the smoked turkey for my brothers and myself, and we share it before dinner when no one can see us.

Many people are put off the by the strong "fishy" flavor of the oily fishes like bluefish. But when they are hot smoked, the flavor of the smoke balances perfectly with the briny flavor of the fish, and the natural oils of the fish keep it nice and moist.

The most-worked muscles in birds depend on whether they're farm raised or wild; either the legs or the wings do the bulk of the work and have the most connective tissue and flavor. Farm-raised poultry do not fly much, if at all, so their legs do the most work, as they scurry around eating bugs, worms, and grass. Wild birds spend most of their energy and work on flight, and so the wings are the hardest-working muscles. In either case, wild or farm raised, the breast meat is the most tender and has the least flavor. I rarely smoke just one cut of poultry — rather, I tend to smoke whole birds (the exception is smoked duck breast; see page 109).

OILY FISH AND WHITE FISH

I don't think of fish in terms of cuts. But it is worth being aware of the differences between oily fish and white fish. Oily fish are those like herring, mackerel, bluefish, salmon, and trout.

These are fish associated with colder waters and tend to have a stronger (fishier) flavor. They are referred as oily fish because they have oil throughout their tissue — a fillet of oily fish may contain up to 30 percent oil. These tend to be my favorite fish for smoking because I like the contrast of the fish flavor with the smoke, and the fattier/oilier fish is especially tasty when smoked. White fish are those like cod or haddock, or flatfish like halibut or flounder. These have white flesh and a mild flavor. Both white fish and oily fish can be either hot or cold smoked.

Smoked haddock is part of the fabric of life in Scotland, and for good reason. This relatively mild, firm-fleshed white fish takes on a nice smoky flavor.

COLLAGEN AND FAT ADD FLAVOR

As I went through the various sections and cuts on the animals, you might have noticed that I sometimes mentioned various levels of heat and times. You may have also noticed that the tougher the cuts are, the longer the smoke times and the lower the cooking temperatures are. Why is that? How does a shoulder go from being a tough piece of muscle to silky, tender meat? The key is in the collagen — the primary connective tissue. Understanding the properties of collagen is essential to understanding how to successfully hot smoke some of our favorite cuts like pork shoulder and beef brisket.

COOKING LOW AND SLOW FOR MOIST, TENDER MEAT

At the heart of the transformation from tough to tender is a chemical process called hydrolysis. Hydrolysis is a process in which the addition of water acts to break down a chemical bond. In the case of collagen, the application of heat *and* water breaks down collagen into gelatin — the sticky substance that is used to thicken sauces, desserts, and traditional glue. The tougher the collagen, the longer it will take to break down into gelatin, which is why we smoke a brisket for so much longer than a ham. Hydrolysis of collagen begins as its temperature rises above 122°F (50°C), but once the temperature rises above 140°F (60°C), the collagen begins to shrink, squeezing the muscle fibers and causing them to expel liquid. The higher the temperature and the faster it rises, the tighter the collagen twists and the more moisture the muscle loses. So, when hydrolysis happens too quickly, you're left with dense, dry meat — not what you want to be serving to your friends and loved ones. But when the muscle is slowly heated to above 122°F (50°C), the collagen breaks down into gelatin, the muscle maintains moisture, and you end up with that classic fall-apart meat. That's why it's so important to *slowly* cook your pork shoulder, beef brisket, and other tougher cuts, and why those cuts are perfectly suited for low and slow hot smoking.

FAT FOR FLAVOR AND MOUTHFEEL

Fat serves three primary purposes in an animal: to insulate the body, to protect the body and vital organs, and to store energy. That last purpose is what makes fat so important to the experience of flavor. Fat cells store energy in the form of fatty acids, as well as storing substances that are fat soluble (any compound that dissolves in fat). As the animal gathers energy from its food, the fat-soluble compounds from the food are stored within the fat cells. That's why animals with a more varied diet — such as those raised on pasture — have more complex and better flavor profiles.

Fat also plays a role in tenderness and general mouthfeel. While fibers like collagen dry out when cooked, fat melts. The melted fat turns to a liquid, adding moisture to the drying fibers, keeping the meat moist as you cook it. It also lubricates the bundles of fibers in the muscles, making it easier for your teeth to separate them, resulting in more succulent meat. This is why a shoulder has a silkier, softer texture than the hind leg does when it's cooked properly, even though the shoulder has much more connective tissue; it also has much more fat. Not only does fat affect texture, but it also affects flavor. As fats melt, they release the aromatic fat-soluble compounds stored in the fats, adding more complex notes to the flavor of the meat.

When you cook the shoulder for a long time at a low temperature, as happens in hot smoking, the connective tissue breaks down and the fat melts. The fat keeps the meat from drying out, while the connective tissue turns to gelatin, giving pulled pork that lip-smacking texture.

PASTURED MEAT

My entrance into professional food production was influenced by reading the work of people like Michael Pollan, Wendell Berry, and Dan Barber. Part of my drive to be a butcher was wanting to help rebuild a sustainable and locally based system of food production. I strongly believe that we should eat less meat, and that the meat we do eat should come from farmers in our region who are raising animals in the open, on pasture and in wooded lots.

My wife, Silka, and I buy most of our pork from our friends at North Plain Farm in Great Barrington, Massachusetts, a diversified livestock farm that includes a dairy operation. The pigs move through various lots and pasture depending on the time of year and the needs of the farm. Sometimes the pigs are in densely wooded areas with lots of oak trees, and sometimes they are in open pasture cleaning up after the chickens and cows. Silka and I are always marveling over the different flavors we taste in our pork chops. Sometimes we taste intense nuttiness, while other times we can taste the sweet and clean flavor of cow's milk. As the seasons change, so does the flavor of the pork. It is just one of things we love about buying meat from our friends and neighbors.

In many of the books about smoking, especially when it comes to barbecue, there is a bias against using grass-fed beef and pastured pork. Pastured meats do develop differently than meat from conventionally raised animals, which are usually fed grain and raised in confinement. There is usually less fat in pastured meat, and the quality of the fat varies depending on the diet and the time of year. There is more collagen in pastured meat, because pastured animals are more physically active. I have found that some recipes or instructions for smoking

conventionally raised meat don't always translate well to pastured meat, and that pastured meat often takes longer to smoke because there is more collagen to break down. I have also talked to people who don't like the stronger flavors associated with pastured meat. But that doesn't mean pastured meat isn't good for smoking. Humans have been smoking pastured (and wild) meat for millennia; we have been smoking conventional meat for less than a century. It might take more experimentation and exploration, but that's the fun part anyway, isn't it?

3

RUBS, BRINES, AND CURES

Although a good cut of meat is essential for a great finished product, there is another essential step before the meat is ready to go in the smoker. Whether we're hot smoking or cold smoking, we always apply salt to the meat, usually in combination with sugar, spices, and herbs. This can be applied in the form of a cure, a wet brine, or a simple rub.

Salting the meat is a crucial step for two reasons. First, the application of salt helps prevent the growth of potentially dangerous bacteria, which is especially important when you're cold smoking. The preservative effects of salt come from its ability to draw out the moisture from the meat, which limits the ability of microbes to grow. This gives an opportunity for enzymes within the meat to break down the proteins and fats into smaller molecules that, over time, release a complex array of flavors in the meat, from citrusy to nutty. This is the second important role salt plays: to enhance the flavor and texture of the meat.

THE RUB

Hot smoking, for the most part, is about giving meat that delicious smoky flavor, not about preserving the meat (though hot smoking does delay the onset of spoilage and reduces the presence of harmful microorganisms). Therefore, applying a cure to the meat isn't strictly necessary. But we still apply a rub before smoking because it helps make the meat taste and look great by creating a delicious crunchy "bark" — the pellicle that attracts and adheres smoke (see Creating a Pellicle, page 30). I always try to have a quart container of basic rub (see page 88) in my pantry (it keeps for a few months). When I'm getting ready to smoke, I start with the basic rub and add other spices to suit what I'm smoking.

I am very free-form with my rubs. I use a large amount of salt and black pepper (usually in a one-to-one ratio), then I add whatever else strikes my fancy: sweet paprika, cayenne, garlic powder, cumin. It depends on what kinds of flavors I'm looking to create and the type of meat I'm smoking. When I add more seasonings to my rub, generally they do not amount to more than half the amount of black pepper in my mixture. So if I have 1 cup of basic rub, it should contain about ½ cup of pepper, which means I would add no more than ¼ cup of herbs abd spices like paprika or garlic powder.

If you're experimenting and want to test the flavor of your rub before covering a large piece of meat with it, try it out on something smaller and quicker first, like a small steak or a pork chop. Put the rub on a chop, sear it in a pan with oil, then finish it off in the oven. Taste it and see if it's what you want or if you need to make some changes to the rub.

I usually apply the rub to a piece of meat an hour before I put it in the smoker, leaving it outside the fridge, so the meat can come to room temperature. When I first started out, I applied rub with too heavy a hand, making the bark somewhat inedible (way too salty). To this day I am still surprised by how light a coat of rub is needed; a good rule is 1 tablespoon of rub per pound of meat.

Applying a rub to meat before hot smoking adds flavor and helps to develop a pellicle. It also results in a delicious, crunchy "bark" layer when the meat is smoked.

BRINING

Brining or wet curing is the technique for curing a piece of meat in a saline solution, usually with herbs, spices, and sugar added to it. It's a great technique for foods that will be hot smoked or cold smoked. Brining can seem somewhat counterintuitive, but it is a wonderful way to cure meat while adding moisture to it. Brining works especially well with poultry, which has a fairly low fat content and can easily dry out during smoking. Pork is another great and typical meat to brine; many types of ham and bacon are brined. Some people like to brine fish, although I tend to use a dry cure for it because I like the drier, firmer texture that results from dry curing. Beef, lamb, and goat can be brined as well, although it is not as common. The most well-known brined beef dish is corned beef.

Brining, just like dry curing, works using the principle of osmosis. The salt from the saline solution enters the meat and disrupts the protein structure, causing the normally tight-fitting sheaths around the muscle cells to relax. This reaction creates space within the muscle structure for the saline solution to enter. The moisture is then retained in the muscle, usually adding about 10 percent in weight to the meat. This allows you to start cooking the meat at a higher moisture content than you would have without brining, resulting in a moister finished product, as well as enhancing the flavor of the meat.

Brining is also a great way to impart more flavors into the meat. The flavors of the herbs and spices in a brine are carried into the meat along with the salt and are much more pronounced in the finished product than they would be in a product that was cured with a dry cure mix, because those flavors are able penetrate the meat much more successfully.

START WITH A BASIC BRINE

When you first start experimenting with brining, it's a good idea to stick to the basic brine ratio of ¾ cup (250 grams) salt to 1 gallon (4 liters)

Brining is an important technique for smoking, especially for poultry and hams. It allows you to infuse the meat with tons of flavor as well as helping it retain moisture during the smoking process.

water (see the recipe on page 92). But once you've become comfortable with the process and have a sense of what you want out of your brine (more salt, less salt, different levels for different ingredients), it's good to be able to calculate your own brine percentage of salt to liquid. To figure out that percentage, take the weight of the salt you're using and divide that by the total weight of the water, and then multiply that number by 100. This is a good example of why it's best to work in metric: 1 liter of water weighs 1 kilogram. For our basic brine, the formula would be 250 grams (141 ounces) salt ÷ 4000 grams (1.05 gallons) water x 100 = 6.25 percent. Sometimes with poultry I like to go lower (my poultry brine is 5.6 percent salt), and with pork I sometimes like to go a little higher (the holiday ham brine on page 99 is a 7.5 percent brine). But, generally speaking, a brine of about 6 percent is what you want to use.

BOIL, COOL, ADD MEAT

The best way to create a brine solution is to mix the water, salt, sugar, and aromatics and bring the solution to a boil, stirring until the salt and sugar are dissolved. This ensures that the salt and sugar are fully dissolved in an efficient manner, while also allowing the aromatics to more deeply flavor the water. Think of it as a kind of tea. Cool the brine to 40°F (4°C) before adding the meat; putting uncooked meat in a hot or warm brine solution risks partially cooking the meat, as well as inviting all kinds of foodborne pathogens to develop.

Speed it up! Here's a trick to help speed things along if you don't want to wait for your brine to come down to temperature. Start out with half of the water called for when bringing the brine to a boil. Once the brine has boiled and the salt and sugar are dissolved, take it off the heat. Pour the solution into whatever container you will be brining in, then put in the rest of the water, in the form of ice cubes, weighing out enough ice to equal the weight of the water you started with. For example, if you started with 2 liters of water, you would add 2 kilograms of ice. This brings the temperature down and adds the correct amount of water.

HOW TO CHOOSE A BRINING VESSEL

For any type of curing, it's best to work in a nonreactive container — essentially, any material except aluminum, cast iron, or copper. I use a large brining bucket made of hard, food-safe plastic; I bought it from an online butcher supply store, and it's specifically made for brining. You can also brine in a large enamel or stainless-steel pot or a large glass container.

Choose a vessel that is large enough for the meat to fit in, but not so snug that the meat will be pressed up against the sides. You want enough space so that the entire surface of the meat is in direct contact with the brine solution. If the meat is pressed against the side of the vessel, the brine won't be able to penetrate as well. You also want to make sure the meat is completely submerged. I often put a plate on top of the meat, with something on the plate to weight it down — a heavy can or jar of food, or even a brick wrapped in plastic wrap. Keep in mind that it all needs to be refrigerated while brining, so choose a container that will fit in your fridge. This can be tricky when you're brining a 20-pound turkey or a 15-pound ham. In the fall and winter, I sometimes keep my brine bucket on the porch, knowing that as long as it stays below 42°F (6°C), it will be okay. The brine solution has enough salinity that it is unlikely to freeze.

HOW LONG TO BRINE

The next question is, how do you know how long to brine something for? I have yet to come up with, nor have I seen, a good basic rule for this that works across all types of meat. But here's what works for me:

- Whole chickens: 8 to 12 hours

- Whole turkeys: 24 hours for 10 to 15 pounds; 24 to 36 hours for 15 to 20 pounds

- Pork: 12 hours per pound

- Beef, lamb, goat: 24 hours per pound

Once you become comfortable with the process, play with it and see what you like. The longer you leave meat in the brine, the saltier it will become. The briefer the time you leave it in, the less salty it will be; with larger cuts of meat, like a ham, you risk not having the brine completely penetrate it. Once the meat is fully brined, remove it from the vessel and throw away the brine. It's tempting to reuse the brine, but this is not a good idea; you run the risk of making yourself and others sick.

AIR-DRY BEFORE SMOKING

Before the meat is ready to be smoked, there is one final step. After being in a brine or dry cure for a period of time, the surface of the meat will be very moist. A wet surface on your meat will not allow the smoke to penetrate; instead you will end up with a black film on your meat and not a very smoky flavor. To avoid this, place the meat on a wire cooling rack in your fridge, uncovered, for at least 12 hours to air-dry. You want the surface of the meat to be slightly tacky to the touch, or as we call it in the smoking world, to have a "pellicle" (see Creating a Pellicle, page 30). Then you are ready to smoke.

WHEN TO USE A BRINE INJECTOR

If you think you might end up brining a lot of larger hams and bone-in cuts of meat, it might be worth buying a brine injector. This is basically a large metal syringe that allows you to inject the brine deep into the tissue, ensuring that the brine penetrates all the way. There is nothing more disappointing than brining and smoking a ham only to cut it open to see a large gray area at the center of the ham, indicating that the brine did not penetrate fully.

The best method for using a brine injector is to find the ends of the ham where the ham bone is and start at one of the ends. Fill the injector with brine and place the injector in the ham as deep as you can, or until you hit the bone (the idea is to ensure that the brine reaches the center of the ham around bone). Repeat every 2 inches, moving along the length of the bone, until you reach the other end of the ham.

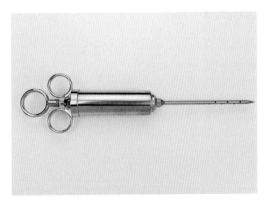

A brine injector is helpful for ensuring that the brine reaches the very center of a ham.

CREATING A PELLICLE

Whether you're hot smoking or cold smoking meat, it's important to create a condition on the surface of the meat that is conducive to allowing the smoke to stick. You need to create a "pellicle" — a tacky, uneven surface. The application of a dry cure or rub, among other things, helps to create a pellicle.

Dry cure. After taking the meat out of a dry cure, gently rinse it with cold water and give it a quick and vigorous rubdown with a clean cloth. Place on a wire rack set in a sheet pan and let rest in your fridge, uncovered, for at least 12 hours and no more than 24 hours before smoking.

Brine. If you've brined your meat first, it's important to let the meat air-dry for at least 12 hours, and no more than 24 hours. If the surface of the meat is too wet, the smoke particles will attach to the moisture on the surface, rather than penetrating the meat, creating a blackish-brown slime that then rubs off.

Rub. The application of a rub is enough to create a good pellicle on its own.

The pork tenderloin at the top hasn't had a cure applied to it; it remains moist, like most fresh meat feels. The tenderloin below it has had a rub applied to it and rinsed off. The surface is now tacky to the touch and the color has changed — an effect of the cure and oxidization. The tenderloin itself is firmer, as it has lost water content.

DRY CURE

"Cured meats" are those that have been salted, smoked, and/or dried. Curing is a process that came out of a need to preserve meat before the advent of refrigeration, but today it is mostly used to produce gourmet food like prosciutto or gravlax. In the context of this book, "cured meats" refers to meat that is salted and smoked, such as lox (salmon), country ham, speck, and some types of dried sausage and bacon.

START WITH SALT

Whether a cured product is simply dried or smoked and dried, the curing process always begins with salting the meat. "The cure," as we call it, is generally a salt mixture made up of table salt (sodium chloride), curing salt (sodium nitrite or nitrate), sugar, and a combination of spices and herbs, in a specific ratio and applied for a specific period of time as dictated by the weight of the meat. Because most cured meats do not get cooked, applying the right amount of cure for the right amount of time is crucial for food safety. Not doing so could cause spoilage and allow for dangerous bacteria and other microbes to develop in the meat.

When you're mixing up a cure, base the amount (in weight) of table salt on 2 to 3 percent of the weight of the meat, and follow the manufacturer's directions for the amount of curing salt (for example, Veg Stable 504 — the industry standard of naturally derived curing salts — calls for using an amount equal to 0.5 percent of the weight of the meat). How long the meat sits in the cure depends on the weight; 1 day per 2 pounds (1 kilogram) ensures that the salt fully penetrates the meat and the right amount of moisture has been removed.

HOW SALT AFFECTS THE MEAT

In addition to removing moisture, the addition of salt creates an environment that is inhospitable to the bacteria that cause spoilage, while also encouraging the growth of microbes that

When applying cure to meat, make sure to coat the entire surface area. When curing salmon, apply a heavier coating over the thickest part of the fillet, to help ensure an even cure.

preserve the meat and enhance the flavor. The inclusion of sugar in a cure helps to balance out the flavor of the salt and also helps to draw out moisture. Enzymes within the meat begin to break down the sugars and release lactic and acetic acids. These acids begin to break down proteins and fats into smaller molecules like peptides. Over time, these peptides turn into flavor compounds that further enhance the flavor of the meat.

The cure also begins to alter the texture and appearance of the meat. The concentration of salt within the meat loosens the protein strands in the muscle cells, causing them to separate. This results in a silkier texture in the meat. The

best example of the effects of cure on meat is prosciutto or jamón. Prosciutto (if you are Italian) or jamón (if you are Spanish) is a ham that is cured with table salt, and sometimes a little sugar and other spices, and hung to dry for a minimum of one year. Many people (myself included) consider it the king of cured meats. (See Tasting the Effects of the Cure, below)

HANG, DRY, SMOKE

After the meat has cured long enough, you can either let it hang to dry in an environment that is around 55°F (13°C) and around 75 percent humidity, or you can smoke it. Smoking helps preserve the meat by allowing it to dry further; the smoke itself also has preservative effects. And as we all know, smoke adds another flavor dimension.

Because curing is about preserving uncooked meat, we generally cold smoke the meat after it's been in cure, rather than hot smoking it. Notable exceptions to this are some kinds of bacon, ham, and sausage. With cold smoking, temperatures don't rise above 90°F (32°C), whereas hot smoking smokes and cooks the meat in a temperature range between 175° and 275°F (80° and 135°C). See chapter 4 for more on smoking methods, and see page 140 for a basic cure recipe.

TASTING THE EFFECTS OF THE CURE: JAMÓN

Envision a plate of thinly sliced prosciutto or jamón. You take a slice and hold it up before you. The light shines through it like it's stained glass, an effect that results from the restructuring of the protein strands while the meat is curing. (Uncured meat would remain opaque.)

You place the slice on your tongue and close your eyes, taking in the flavors. You might taste something nutty, maybe a hint of Parmesan, probably something akin to cantaloupe or possibly apple, maybe grass, and some butter. These flavors could only come through because of the process of curing, where the salt removes the water content and concentrates the flavor, while simultaneously creating chemical breakdowns (the enzymes breaking down the proteins and fat cells) that release these hidden flavors (the peptides). Now that your mouth is abuzz with unexpected flavors, you start to chew and the prosciutto virtually melts in your mouth, barely requiring any chewing. This is another result of the restructuring of the protein strands that occurs from the introduction of salt.

HIMALAYAN
PINK SALT

SEL GRIS

KOSHER SALT

SMOKED SALT

A PRIMER ON SELECTING SALT

How do you know which kind of salt to use? The first distinction we need to make is between table salt (sodium chloride) and *curing* salt (sodium nitrate). We'll focus on table salt first and discuss curing salt next.

For salting meat for smoking and curing, I use either kosher salt or a natural fine white sea salt, simply because they are low in naturally occurring minerals (which could affect the flavor of the cure; look for salt with less than 1 percent other minerals), they don't have any chemical additives, and they have a consistent grain size (which makes it easier to measure salt in a consistent way). A fine-grain salt will ensure a good, even coating on the meat surface; it also ensures that the salt dissolves evenly and consistently. For this reason, I use a natural fine sea salt that I buy in 50-pound bags from my local food co-op.

WHAT ABOUT KOSHER SALT?

You may have noticed that many recipes, especially for working with meat, call for kosher salt. It's called "kosher salt" not because it *is* kosher, but because it's used to kosher meat — a process that involves drawing the blood out of the meat. Kosher salt is often called for in cooking with meat because it is a relatively pure salt (only sodium chloride), it has been through a process to remove other minerals, and it doesn't have iodine added to it (something most other table salts have). Although you don't need to use kosher salt, you should find a salt that does not have iodine or anti-caking agents added — both of which are common in table salt.

SAVE THE ARTISANAL SALTS FOR FINISHING

Recently, there has been increased interest in artisanal salts from all over the world, with various colors, textures, and flavors: red, black, gray, white, chunky, flaky, round, or flat. These salts are not further processed once they're mined or harvested (from evaporated sea water). The colors and shapes reflect the various other minerals in the crystals and the natural crystal shapes they form. While these salts are fascinating and fun to use, they're best used as a finishing salt — to have on the table to sprinkle on a dish once it is cooked and ready to eat. Using artisanal salts on your meats in preparation for smoking is risky, because the naturally occurring minerals found in them can have unexpected effects on your meat. Not only that, the non-uniform shape of the crystals can lead them to dissolve unevenly, which adds more unpredictability to the process.

CURE #1

VEG STABLE 504

CURE #2

CURING SALTS

Curing salts (sodium nitrite) serve an entirely different purpose than table salt does. Including curing salt in your cure or brine is important when making bacon, hams, or anything that is to be cold smoked. First, nitrites kill a wide range of bacteria, most importantly the one responsible for botulism. Second, nitrites help preserve the meat. The nitrogen bonds with the hemoglobin in the meat, acting as an antioxidant and thus stopping the oxidization of the meat. Oxidization causes meat to become brown or gray and increases the rate at which the meat goes rancid. Third, nitrites add a distinct flavor to the meat that I can best describe as "hammy" — a certain kind of piquant umami.

There are essentially two types of curing salt available: pink salts and plant-derived sodium nitrate powders.

PINK SALTS

Pink salts are synthetically produced and are dyed pink to avoid confusing them with table salt. The pink dye has nothing to do with the fact that nitrites help meat stay reddish pink. The two types of pink salt are called curing salt #1 and curing salt #2.

Curing salt #1. This is also called "Prague powder #1" or "Insta Cure #1" and is a combination of sodium nitrite and sodium chloride. It's used for products that are cured for a shorter amount of time and are cooked, like most hams, bacon, and hot-smoked sausages.

Curing salt #2. Also known as "Prague powder #2" or "Insta Cure #2," it is a combination of sodium nitrite, sodium nitrate, and sodium chloride. The sodium nitrates break down over time into sodium nitrites, which is why they are used in products that are cured over a long period of time, like jamón, prosciutto, speck, and dry-cured sausages. You can use Cure #1 as a substitute for Cure #2, but you should not use Cure #2 as a substitute for Cure #1.

PLANT-DERIVED SODIUM NITRITES

Then there are vegetable powders that contain sodium nitrites derived from plants. Plants like celery are juiced and then fermented to transform some of their nitrates to nitrite. After the juice is fermented, it is dried, and then its nitrite content is measured. Once the nitrite content is determined, the powder is standardized by adding sodium chloride to it. You can find this sold as celery powder (not to be confused with celery salt) or Veg Stable 504 (sometimes listed as Veg Cure 504 or Veg Powder 504). Plant-derived sodium nitrites can be used as a substitute for both Cure #1 and Cure #2.

ARE CURING SALTS SAFE?

There is a lot of confusion and misunderstanding about the use of sodium nitrites and a sense that sodium nitrates and nitrates are a harmful, unnecessary additive to meat. To be clear: salt with nitrites in it has been used to cure meat for over a millennium. Anthropological evidence tells us that originally people used saltpeter, or potassium nitrate, for curing meats. In the last century, most people switched to sodium nitrite because it is more consistent in its results than potassium nitrate. Sodium nitrites are a naturally occurring compound that are found in greens like spinach, kale, chard, and celery. There is evidence that sodium nitrites are a carcinogen when consumed in large quantities, but that risk is negligible in a well-balanced, normal diet.

You can buy bacon, ham, salami, and other meats that are labeled "uncured" or "no nitrites added." However, these products *do* still have nitrites added to them; the nitrites are just in the form of a dehydrated vegetable like celery. This only adds to the confusion of consumers, unfortunately. Whether the nitrites come from a naturally occurring source like vegetables or are produced in a lab like pink salt, the USDA will not allow processors to produce cured meats without the presence of sodium nitrites.

When weighing the benefits of including nitrites in smoked and cured meats versus the potential risks of not using them, I side on including them. For me, the risk of botulism and spoiled meat outweighs the relatively low risk of heart disease and cancer. That said, I do prefer using naturally occurring nitrites derived from vegetables like celery, chard, or kale, simply out of a preference to use natural ingredients (though there is no conclusive evidence these nitrites are less harmful than those that are synthetically produced). In my own smoking and curing, I use Veg Stable 504.

HONEY & GARLIC BACON
(No Nitrites or Nitrates Added,* Uncured, Smoked Bacon)

Ingredients: Pork Belly, Honey, Sea Salt, Garlic, Vegetable Juice Powder
*No nitrites or nitrates added except those that exist naturally in vegetables and sea salt
Net W
Produced for Jackiscooking LLC, Ancramdale NY 12503

TURBINADO

MUSCOVADO

MAPLE SUGAR

SUGAR

Just using salt on meat to cure it can create a slightly harsh flavor. The exception is dry-cured products like jamón or prosciutto that are aged for a long time to allow the meat to mellow out. The most common way to balance out the salt is to add a form of sugar. Not only does sugar help balance the effect of the salt, but it has similar antimicrobial properties. In dry-cured meats, it helps in the preservation process, feeding the microbes that produce natural acids in the meat.

FLAVOR PROFILES OF VARIOUS SWEETENERS

Different sugar sources create different effects; each one has unique flavors and properties.

WHITE SUGAR

White sugar is a refined version of raw sugar, which itself is created from the juice of sugarcane or sugar beets. The refining process removes the molasses, resulting in the granulated white crystals we are all familiar with. It provides a very clean, sweet flavor.

BROWN SUGARS

These are also granulated sugars, but ones that have not had all of the molasses removed. Some lower-quality brown sugars are actually refined white sugar that has some molasses reintroduced. Turbinado and demerara are made from crystallized, partially evaporated sugarcane juice, which is then spun in a centrifuge to remove most of the molasses. Muscovado is not centrifuged; it's produced by slowly cooking down cane syrup until it becomes crystallized. This process leaves more molasses and other minerals in the sugar, which is why muscovado is usually darker in color and stronger in flavor. Its full, earthy flavor, which I love, lends itself well to smoked pork and salmon in particular.

BROWN SUGAR

WHITE SUGAR

HONEY

SORGHUM

MAPLE SYRUP

MOLASSES

MOLASSES

This syrup, a by-product of sugar refining, is what gives brown sugar its distinctive color and flavor. It was very popular in colonial American cooking and was also an important ingredient in British curing and smoking traditions, where it is called "treacle."

Molasses comes in three types, corresponding to what stage of the process they come from. The first boiling is called first syrup or cane syrup and is the lightest. The second is called second syrup and comes from the second boiling and sugar extraction; this is darker and thicker, and it has a slightly bitter flavor. The third is blackstrap molasses, and it comes from the third boiling. It is the thickest and darkest and has the most

robust flavor of the three types. Blackstrap is very high in minerals and fairly low in sugar content. I love the flavor of blackstrap and often use it in my hams and sometimes my bacons. It's a popular ingredient in American Southern and British curing and smoking for products like blackstrap country hams and Wiltshire hams. It is also a great ingredient in barbecue sauces.

MAPLE SYRUP

Maple syrup is produced by collecting the sap of sugar maples, red maples, and black maples and boiling it down to evaporate the water content. To create maple sugar, which is granulated, the syrup is boiled until it crystallizes. Maple sugar and syrup tend to have a cleaner taste than brown sugars, but with a distinctive flavor. Maple is another great sugar for bacons and hams.

SORGHUM

Sorghum is a sugar that's popular in the South, where the plant originates. Like molasses, it is a syrup, rather than a granulated sugar. Like sugarcane, sorghum is also a grass, and its syrup is produced in a way similar to molasses. The plant's juice is extracted by cutting, crushing, or mashing, and then it's boiled down to a golden syrup that has a sweet, earthy flavor.

SUGAR-FREE BACON?

In the last few years, I've encountered a lot of customers who ask me for bacon without sugar. The basis for this request is reasonable. In general, we consume way too much sugar, and it is needlessly added to many processed foods. We have come to learn how terrible this has been for our health. Many of the more recent diet trends have called for the elimination of sugar, especially refined sugar, from your diet. Fortunately, there are many great non-refined sugars available, each one with its own interesting flavor profile.

The truth is, for most cured meat we need sugar in order for it to taste good. The sugar balances out the harshness of the salt that is required to make cured meats safe. While it's good to be wary of excess sugar in your diet, in the case of smoking and curing meats it's actually essential for producing a delicious piece of food.

HONEY

Honey is produced by bees from the nectar of flowers. Depending on which nectar the bees collect, you can get a wide range of colors and flavors, including wildflower, citrus, clover, buckwheat, and tupelo. I'm partial to buckwheat and tupelo, which have darker, earthier flavors. That said, when I'm using honey in curing and smoking, I tend to stick to milder ones like wildflower or clover. I often use honey in brines for poultry and pork, in bacon cures (I make a honey-garlic bacon and a miso-honey bacon; see page 143), as well as in glazes for hams.

SPICES AND HERBS

Most recipes call for the addition of spices and herbs to your salt mixture, and these ingredients bring other flavors to the meat. There is no hard rule about which spices and herbs you can use in your recipes; this is a place where you can play around and be creative. That said, there are certain spices and herbs that are traditionally blended together, and it's worth being aware of these and using them as your jumping-off point. For instance, in Spain, smoked paprika and garlic are used together; in northern Italy a common blend includes rosemary, bay leaves, and juniper.

FRESHER IS BETTER

Herbs can be used either fresh or dried. I prefer to use fresh ones, because the flavor is brighter, but there's nothing wrong with using dried herbs. When substituting one for the other, use a ratio of two to one, fresh to dried.

If you do choose to use dried herbs, freshness is still important. This is also true with dried spices. Nothing lasts forever, and as these ingredients age, they lose their potency. Because of that, it's best to buy spices in small amounts from the bulk section of your local grocery store, so that they don't linger on your spice rack for years.

One way to keep your spices tasting vibrant is by buying them whole and grinding them yourself. While preground spices are convenient, there is a real difference in flavor in spices you grind yourself. The difference between whole coriander seed that is freshly ground, for example, and the preground stuff is astonishing. Either way, whole or ground, spices and dried herbs should be kept in sealed containers in a cool, dark place.

CLASSIC SPICE AND HERB PROFILES

Bay leaves. Highly aromatic, with a sweet, herbal, piney scent and slightly bitter taste. Commonly used in the cuisine of the Alpine region and great in stocks.

Black pepper. Spicy, pungent, and slightly smoky.

Cayenne. This is a type of chile that is usually finely ground. It is moderately hot with a piquant flavor. It is a great way to inject heat into your food and used in many recipes.

Clove. Warm and sweet, with a slightly bitter flavor. Use sparingly.

Coriander. The seeds are earthy but bright and lemony. Great with pork, beef, lamb, or goat.

Cumin. Earthy, nutty, slightly sweet, and a little smoky. Often used in concert with coriander (especially in Southeast Asian, Indian, Middle Eastern, North African, and Mexican cooking). Great with pork, beef, lamb, or goat.

Fennel. Sweet, aromatic licorice flavor. Seeds are a key ingredient in a lot of Italian curing.

Garlic. Pungent, sharp, sweet, and spicy.

Ginger. Sweet, spicy, and warming. Adds a nice brightness. Goes well with any meat.

Juniper. Bittersweet, with a clean flavor. A great spice to use with pork.

Mace. Delicate, fragrant, warm, sweet, and slightly smoky. Gives Jamaican jerk its distinctive flavor. Great with pork, goat, or lamb. Use sparingly.

Nutmeg. A flavor profile similar to mace (they're from the same plant), just a little more bitter. Use in small amounts. Brings out the natural sweetness of pork.

Paprika. Can be sweet, spicy/hot, or smoked. (It is also called pimentón in Spanish cuisine, where it is a key ingredient.)

Red pepper flakes. Spicy and often fruity. (There are myriad pepper flakes! My favorites are Calabrian, ancho, Thai, and de arbol.)

Rosemary. Fragrant, piney, and slightly bitter. Wonderful with pork.

Sage. Fragrant and piney. Great with poultry and pork.

Thyme. Fragrant, floral, and light. Great with all meats.

White pepper. Milder than black pepper, with a slightly musty aroma.

Yellow mustard seed. Spicy, pungent, and a little bitter, with subtle heat.

GARLIC

PEPPER FLAKES

ALLSPICE

ROSEMARY

CORIANDER

BLACK PEPPERCORNS

PAPRIKA

MACE

GINGER

YELLOW MUSTARD SEED

NUTMEG

SAGE

BAY

FENNEL

THYME

CAYENNE

4

HEAT AND SMOKE

- -

*T*his is what it's all about: the smoke. Aromatic and flavorful, smoke is nothing more than a collection of solid particulates, liquid, and gases that are emitted from the burning of a material — most often wood.

- -

In the context of this book, you use smoke to flavor food, and often to preserve it, usually by generating smoke in an enclosed area that also holds the food. The process by which the smoke is generated, the source of the smoke, the object or objects in which to generate the smoke and hold the food, and the temperature at which the food is held while smoking will all vary greatly depending on what you want your end product to be.

There are three points in this process at which you decide about the flavor and texture of your final product. First, you choose what you want to smoke, whether it's whole chicken, a brisket, a pork tenderloin, or another cut. Then you choose which salts, sugars, spices, and herbs you're going to apply to it. Those first two decisions are true for any cooking method. It's the third and final decision that sets smoking apart from any other form of cooking. In this chapter you will learn how smoking temperature and type of fuel affect the final flavor and texture of your smoked food.

CHOOSE YOUR METHOD

The decision of whether to dry cure, brine, or simply apply a rub to your meat is, in great part, informed by your decision of how you'll be smoking the meat. There are two different temperature ranges for smoking — hot and cold. Hot smoking imparts a smoky flavor and fully cooks the food. Cold smoking imparts a smoky flavor and helps to preserve the meat, but it does not cook the meat. Both techniques yield delicious — though very different — results.

Hot smoking — for which the fire and meat are in the same chamber, typically between 175° and 275°F (80° and 135°C) — is a technique that allows you to fully cook the meat while infusing it with a smoky flavor. Hot-smoked products include barbecue, smoked hams, and pastrami.

HOT SMOKING

When we talk about smoking meat, most people imagine hot smoking. Think of your classic smoked brisket or whole hog. Hot smoking occurs when the meat is held directly above or near the heat source and therefore cooks while it is smoked. When hot smoking, you're usually looking for an ambient temperature range between 175° and 275°F (80° and 135°C). This allows the meat to fully cook, lets the smoke penetrate and flavor the meat, and allows the connective tissues in the meat to slowly break down, yielding a delicious, supple, smoky piece of fully cooked meat. Depending on what you're smoking, different recipes will call for different temperature ranges. Hot smoking can usually be done in less than 12 hours.

COLD SMOKING

Cold smoking is more associated with cured meats like speck or country ham and delicate fish like salmon or trout. Cold smoking flavors and preserves the meat but does not cook it. The meat and heat source are set away from each other, usually with the fire in a firebox connected through piping to another chamber where the meat rests, so that the smoke is relatively cool by the time it reaches the meat. Generally speaking, cold smoking occurs in an ambient temperature of 90°F (32°C) or below; the specific temperature range doesn't matter so much, as long as it's below 90°F (32°C). Cold smoking usually takes place for a longer duration than hot smoking, going for days or even weeks. This prolonged exposure to the smoke gives cold-smoked foods a more intense smoky flavor. Because the meat is not cooked, you need to be very careful about food safety. This is why we cure the meat before we smoke it. You should also be aware of the ambient temperature and humidity when cold smoking. The higher the humidity in the air, the harder it is for the smoke to reach and penetrate the meat; the cool, dry weather of fall and winter is best for cold smoking.

Cold smoking gives the product a smoky flavor but doesn't cook it. This is achieved by having the fire in one chamber that is connected via piping to a separate chamber that contains the product. During cold smoking, the temperature is generally kept below 90°F (32°C). This technique is used with cured meats like speck, smoked lox (salmon), and some styles of dry-cured sausages.

CHOOSE YOUR FUEL

Fuel source is another component that greatly affects the outcome of your final product. I have a lot of fun with this part, and I love to experiment. Whenever I build a fire, I pay attention to what I am feeding it. As it burns, I find myself sniffing the air, looking for new aromas. Sometimes just the perfume of the fire will inspire me to combine certain kinds of wood smoke with a certain cut or cure. I also use my simple kettle grill to play with the effects of alternative sources of smoke. This way I don't have to experiment on a 9-pound pork butt that takes 8 hours to smoke to get a sense of the flavor the smoke will impart and how that material will burn. That being said, I recommend that you first get comfortable with the meat, the cure, and the basic smoking temperatures before you start playing with different fuel sources. Start with basic hardwoods, and don't get caught up in trying to find the perfect one — use what you have most easily available to you.

WHICH TYPE OF WOOD?

People tend to have strong opinions about what kind of wood they like to smoke with, as well as which cuts and types of meat go best with which

---

THE PRESERVATIVE EFFECT OF SMOKE

Although curing meat in a salt mixture is an essential step in the process of creating food-safe conditions and preserving the meat, the application of smoke itself also plays an important role in that process. Wood smoke contains many chemicals that slow the growth of microbes, including formaldehyde and acetic acid. Not only does smoke contain antimicrobial chemical compounds, but the pH level of smoke itself (2.5) is also antimicrobial. Many of the phenolic compounds in wood smoke are also antimicrobial, and phenol itself is a disinfectant as well as an antioxidant (which prevents rancidity in meat and fat). As the smoke clings to the surface of the meat, all of these invisible chemical reactions are happening to create a preservative environment. As with the application of cure, the benefits of the smoking process are a better-tasting and safer food product.

BIRCH   **MAPLE**   **CHERRY**   **APPLE**

kinds of smoke. I like the smoke to be another expression of terroir — the characteristic tastes and flavors imparted to a food product by the physical environment in which it is produced. In Jamaica, for instance, part of the distinct flavor of jerk comes from the fact that pimento wood (allspice) is used to fuel the fire. I live in New England, and I use the wood that I have available to me on my land — white oak, maple, black cherry, apple, and birch. Trees and limbs come down every year, and my brother Will and I harvest what we can for our smokehouse. Some years we have a lot of apple; other years it's oak. Usually we also buy some wood from a friend and neighbor who is a logger. Because of the design of my smoker, and my lack of a wood chipper, I use split logs rather than woodchips or sawdust. My brother and many of our friends are woodworkers, so I'll occasionally have bags of sawdust to use — when I can be assured of what kind of wood it is and that it is untreated. I use the sawdust in my grill, upright barrel smoker, donabe, or stove-top smoker.

There are some good general guidelines to follow when you're selecting a source of wood, but there aren't hard-and-fast rules. With that in mind, I encourage you to experiment and see what works best for you. Try doing a smoke with just cherry, and then do one with just oak, to see if you notice a difference, and if you have a preference for one or the other.

Seasoned hardwood. Generally speaking, it's best to smoke with seasoned hardwood — that is, wood from broad-leaved deciduous trees like oak, hickory, maple, fruit trees, and beech. "Seasoned" refers to wood that has been cut and left to air-dry for 6 to 9 months. When wood is first cut down, it's referred to as "green," and it has a moisture content of 50 to 60 percent. Once the wood is seasoned, that drops to about 20 percent. Because of the high moisture content of green wood, its smoke can be very intense, to the point of being acrid. Green wood also takes longer to catch fire and can smolder out, making it harder to control the fire and thus the temperature of the smoker.

Evergreens. Though deciduous hardwood is most common for smoking, there are traditions throughout the world where evergreen wood and needles are used as a source of smoke. Evergreens have a lot of resin in their wood; this creates a smoke that imparts a turpentine flavor and overall generates a dirtier smoke that covers the meat in a sooty black coating. People in Bavaria have been using evergreens — usually fir — to smoke meat for centuries. In fact, it gives us one of the most recognizable smoked products in the world, the Black Forest ham.

In France, there is a wonderful dish that involves smoking mussels in a bed of pine needles. In Canada, where there is an abundance of evergreens, fresh spruce is put in the grill to impart flavor to steaks. I like to add spruce or fir when I am smoking lamb or mutton. And cedar adds fantastic flavor to fish; you can often find cedar planks sold specifically for cooking fish on.

SPLIT LOGS

I love smoking with split logs, but they can be harder to manage than woodchips or sawdust. Smoking with split logs is best suited for larger smokers or when you are smoking in the open air. When I use split logs, it is either in conjunction with my grill table or in my smokehouse — both for cold smoking and hot smoking. It took me a while to learn how to manage the burning of split logs so that the temperature stayed steady and a nice even smoke was produced. The key is to develop a nice bed of coal before you attempt smoking over the split logs. Often, I build a fire an hour or so before I put any meat in the smoker or on the grill. This way the bed of coals works to slowly and steadily burn the split logs, producing an even smoke level and temperature range. One of the great things about using split logs is that once you get them going, they burn for a long time.

WOODCHIPS

Woodchips are another way to experiment with different kinds of wood smoke. I only use woodchips when I am using an electric or propane smoker, my barrel smoker, or my kettle grill. When I use my barrel smoker or kettle grill I start with a pile of hot charcoal and place a layer of woodchips over the charcoal. The charcoal slowly burns the woodchips, producing a nice smoke. Woodchips burn pretty quickly, as opposed to split logs, so I reserve using them for items that require a shorter smoke time. There is also the matter of space. Kettle grills and drum smokers are relatively small, and thus you need to produce less smoke to fill them with smoke. Woodchips work well in this scenario. Anyway, even if you wanted to, you wouldn't be able to fit a bunch of split logs in your kettle grill or drum smoker.

WOOD SHAVINGS   SPLIT HARDWOOD LOG   WOODCHIPS

TO SOAK OR NOT TO SOAK?

When it comes to using woodchips, there is a great debate about whether or not to soak them in water first. Both in my own experimenting and in the opinion of chefs and barbecue professionals I trust, the soaking does not make much of a difference. Soaking the chips gives the *appearance* of generating more smoke, but what you're actually seeing is more steam. This steam can have its own benefits, depending on what you're smoking; it generates more moisture, which can help offset the drying effect of the smoke and temperature. This can be useful for keeping sausage casings from drying out too much, for example.

SAWDUST

Sawdust (or wood shavings) is perfect for stove-top smoking, whether you're using a stainless-steel stove-top smoker or a ceramic donabe. (Though, based on personal experience, I do *not* encourage you to try to smoke a whole ham with sawdust in an oven in a city apartment building.) The principles for using sawdust are similar to those for woodchips. The flame from the stove-top burner acts as the heat source, which is conducted to the sawdust through the vessel you're smoking in. Just as woodchips are less efficient than split logs, sawdust is less efficient than woodchips. They are ideal for very quick-smoked items like fish, poultry, pork chops, or steaks. The sawdust will ignite and slowly burn, generating smoke, which will fill the smoker. You want to create a consistent smolder, adding more sawdust as needed. When smoking indoors, make sure your kitchen is well ventilated.

AVOID TEMPERATURE SPIKES

During the smoking process, you generally want to avoid creating big temperature fluctuations — for example, from adding a large quantity of woodchips all at once. This is harder than it sounds. It took me a while to get a good feel for the rhythm of adding fuel to my smoker. In the beginning, you're bound to have big temperature fluctuations, but don't worry — you'll get the hang of it over time.

STARTING THE FIRE: LOG CABIN STYLE

If you're using split logs for smoking, try starting the fire with the log cabin technique.

2. Make a kindling tepee. Place small pieces of kindling, the thickness of a wooden spoon handle, leaning on the mound of tinder, as if you were building a tiny tepee.

3. Build the cabin. Place a split log on either side of the kindling tepee, leaving about an inch of space between the logs and the tepee. Build up with additional logs as if you were making a log cabin, laying each layer perpendicular to the last, using smaller and smaller logs on each progressive layer. I like to go up three or four levels.

1. Mound the tinder. Make a small, loose mound of tinder — like shavings, small twigs, dried leaves, pine needles, or a few handfuls of crumpled paper.

4. Light it up. Ignite the tinder. Once the log cabin has caught fire and is burning steadily, you can feed the fire as needed to maintain the right temperature.

STARTING THE SMOKE: PILING IT ON

1. Start with hot embers. Generate a bed of hot embers from hardwood lump charcoal.

2. Place a mound of chips on top of the embers. Try to maintain the mound by adding chips, as it encourages them to smolder and smoke, rather than to combust.

3. Steadily add more chips. Add to the mound gradually, maintaining a steady supply of smoke and heat. As with everything in smoking, slow and steady wins the race. The grill and meat can be set in place any time after the chips begin to smoke.

Alder. This is a great wood for smoking fish. It has a light, delicate, and slightly sweet flavor. In the Pacific Northwest, it's commonly used to smoke salmon.

Beech. Similar to oak, it has a mild flavor and burns slowly and evenly. This is a wood that I cut in with others to keep the fire burning consistently.

Birch. Much like maple, birch imparts a slight sweetness. It's a little softer than oak or maple, though, so it doesn't burn for quite as long. I have yet to experiment with a straight black birch smoke, but I am very curious to find out if I can get a birch beer flavor on something mild like poultry or fish.

Fruitwood. This is a wonderful and common fuel for smoking. It lends a slight sweetness and subtle fruity flavor to meat. Cherry can even add a slightly rosy hue to the meat. Because of the subtle flavor of fruitwood smoke, it's perfect for mild meats like fish, poultry, and even pork.

I end up using a fair amount of fruitwood because we live on what was once an orchard, more than a century ago. Our property also has a lot of black cherry trees. So, when old apple or cherry limbs come down, my brother cuts them up with a chainsaw, and we haul them over to the smokehouse woodpile.

Hickory. This is another popular all-around wood, with a very recognizable smell. Many people associate the smell of hickory with good barbecue. It has a slightly stronger flavor than oak, with a more pronounced nutty flavor. Like cherry, it can give the meat a nice rosy color. This is a great wood for food with a stronger flavor profile, like beef or lamb, or for something heavily seasoned. Because it has a slightly more robust flavor than oak, I don't use it for poultry or fish.

Maple. Whether or not it's sugar maple, maple generally has a lot of wood sugar, so it imparts a sweet flavor to the meat. It's on the milder side, so its effects can get lost on strongly flavored food. It also creates a nice steady source of smoke due to the density of the wood.

Mesquite. This is a wood with a lot of allure — maybe a result of nostalgia for the Old West? It has a strong sagebrush-like flavor that can be slightly bitter. The wood burns hot and fast, so it's best used as a flavor source when it has already burned down to coals. I would reserve mesquite for beef.

Oak. This is probably the most commonly used fuel source for smoking. The qualities that make oak a sought-after wood for wine barrels are also what make it sought after for smoking: it gives a slightly woodsy, nutty flavor. It also burns evenly and for a long time, making it a steady source of heat. I use oak for its even heat, in conjunction with another wood for flavor, like apple or cherry.

Old whiskey and wine barrels. Most whiskey and wine barrels are made from oak. Using the used barrels as a source of smoke adds a whole other flavor element, depending on what was aged in the barrel. One of our local distilleries sells chunks of used whiskey barrels specifically for this purpose. If there's someone in your area making whiskey or wine, I recommend befriending them and seeing if you can get your hands on some of their old, broken barrels.

Pecan. Pecan is a member of the hickory family and gives a milder version of the same flavor that hickory produces: slightly sweet and nutty. This is a great wood to use with fish and poultry. If you want to intensify the nutty flavor, throw some pecan shells into the fire.

Walnut. Walnut gives big flavor that can be a little overpowering. Black walnut in particular has high levels of tannin in it and can leave a slightly bitter taste. This is a wood best used for beef, and perhaps not until you feel confident about your smoking skills.

SPRUCE
BRANCHES HAY TEA CORN COBS PINE NEEDLES

OTHER SOURCES OF FUEL

Corn cobs. Smoking with corn cobs is very popular in the American Midwest, where millions of acres are dedicated to growing corn. Cob imparts a sweet grassy aroma. Like hay, corn cobs burn quickly, so you'll need a lot of them; sourcing them might be a challenge if you don't live in the Midwest. If you have a friend or neighbor who grows a lot of corn, approach them about whether they might let you glean their fields after the harvest. I have found that the promise of delivering some morsel of smoked deliciousness as a payback can get you a lot.

Dried dung. This source of smoke has been used for centuries and can have a wonderful effect. Most famously, it's used in Iceland, where both lamb and fish are smoked over dried dung. Wherever this is done, from Iceland to Tibet, the sources of dung are ruminants: cows, sheep, or yaks. Ruminants eat grass, and so it is worth thinking of smoking with dung as a form of smoking with hay, but with an earthier flavor.

Hay. Another great source of smoke is hay. Good hay imparts sweet, barnyard, grassy notes. If you want to experiment with smoking with hay, make sure you're buying certified organic hay, or getting it from a farmer who uses organic methods. I like to use hay with lamb and beef, playing on the barnyard flavor notes inherent in the meat. I use hay much like I would use woodchips, starting with a layer of hot embers and placing the hay on top. Because hay burns so quickly, I usually soak it first.

Tea. In China and Japan, tea is often used for smoking food. Traditionally, black teas like oolong or Ceylon are used, along with jasmine tea. Usually rice is mixed in with the tea to add to the flavor profile. I smoke duck breast with tea (see page 109); it's also perfect for smoking a mild white fish like cod or haddock and for pork belly. Tea should be used as you would use sawdust, for items that require a short smoke time and in smokers that have small volumetric space. I place the tea (and rice) in the bottom of my vessel — usually a donabe, but you could use a wok.

PART 2

CHOOSING A SMOKER

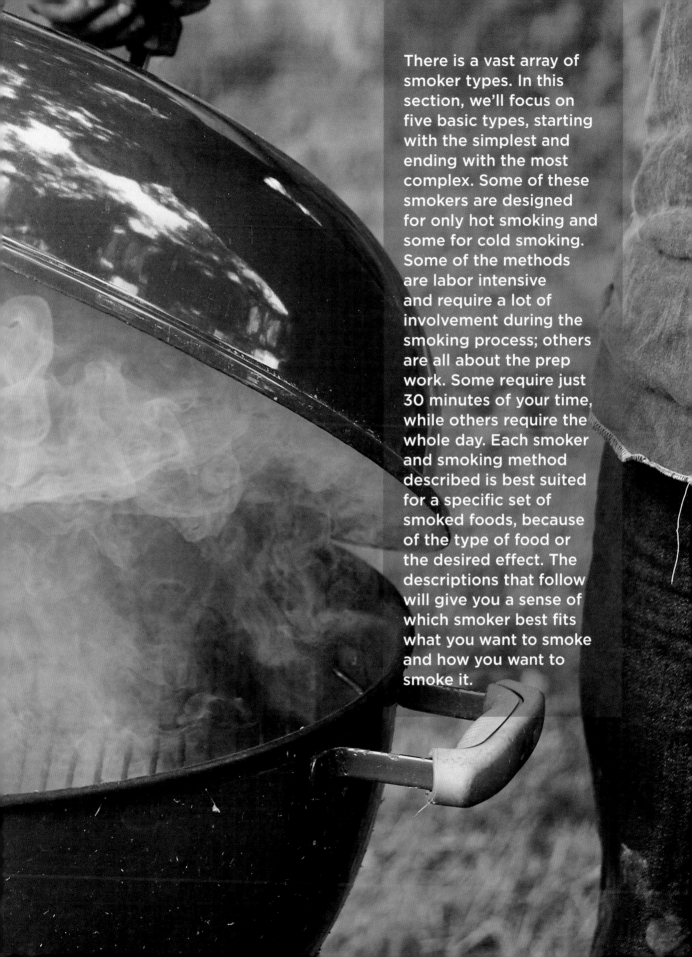

There is a vast array of smoker types. In this section, we'll focus on five basic types, starting with the simplest and ending with the most complex. Some of these smokers are designed for only hot smoking and some for cold smoking. Some of the methods are labor intensive and require a lot of involvement during the smoking process; others are all about the prep work. Some require just 30 minutes of your time, while others require the whole day. Each smoker and smoking method described is best suited for a specific set of smoked foods, because of the type of food or the desired effect. The descriptions that follow will give you a sense of which smoker best fits what you want to smoke and how you want to smoke it.

STOVE-TOP SMOKERS

Let's begin where my smoking adventures did: with the stove-top smoker. Stove-top smoking is best suited for hot smoking smaller cuts of meat that only need a short smoking time — foods like fish, poultry, steaks, pork chops, and tenderloins. Stove-top smokers are a great way to start playing around with smoking without investing a lot of time, energy, or money. It's more than likely that you already have everything you need to put together a stove-top smoker in your kitchen. You can also buy a stove-top smoker, like I did when I first began my smoking adventures years ago, but what's the fun in that? If you're going to try this, make sure you either have a good range hood fan or an otherwise very well-ventilated kitchen, or do it on a hot plate outside.

SMOKING IN A STOVE-TOP POT/KETTLE SMOKER

There is little difference between the stove-top pan smoker and the kettle smoker, other than size and shape. I choose one over the other based on what I am smoking. If I want to smoke several duck breasts, a fillet of salmon, or pork tenderloins, I'll put together a pan smoker (shown above) because a roasting pan can better accommodate those items. If I'm going to smoke a whole chicken or a small roast, I'll put together a kettle smoker to best accommodate their size and shape.

1. Line the bottom of the pot with aluminum foil to protect it, and spread a thin, even layer (about ¼ inch) of wood shavings or sawdust on it.

2. Place the steamer insert in the pot, making sure there is room between the steamer basket and the pot for smoke to flow, and place your food in the steamer basket.

3. Place the pot over high heat for about 5 minutes or until it starts smoking.

4. Place a tight-fitting lid on the pot. Scrunch extra foil around the edges of the lid to ensure that no smoke can escape.

5. Lower the heat to medium-low and cook until the meat reaches the desired temperature (using a wireless thermometer is helpful in this process). Turn off the heat and let the food rest in the smoker for about 10 minutes. Remove the foil and lid. If the meat is cooked through, it's ready to eat right now. If not, transfer it to a sheet pan and finish it in the oven.

ELECTRIC AND GAS SMOKERS

Although pellet, electric, and gas smokers lack a certain romance, they are great tools for someone who loves to smoke food but doesn't have the time to dedicate to an all-day smoking session or to making their own smoker. There are many types of these automatic smokers to choose from, from large-scale professional smokers that you would find in restaurants and commercial smokehouses to small units designed for home enthusiasts.

The beauty of these machines is that you can set them and forget them, without having to worry about keeping the fire going and managing the temperature. You add the required fuel (pellets, woodchips, or sawdust), set the smoker to the desired temperature, and place the food inside. Then you just leave it until the product is done. Some of these smokers even have timer settings, so that they automatically start and/or turn off at the desired time. Some can even be set to change temperatures throughout the cook time. Pellet smokers use little pellets made of compressed sawdust. Other gas and electric smokers use sawdust and or woodchips. I have a small electric smoker that I fuel with woodchips. I use it in the winter months when I don't want to be outside firing up my smokehouse, or on a busy day when I am dying for some ribs, but I can't be home all day tending a fire.

Although I prefer the romance and beauty of my smokehouse, sometimes I don't have the time to spend all day tending a fire. Luckily, on those days I can still get my smoked ribs fix by relying on my little electric smoker. I can set it and forget it, knowing that 4 hours later I will have some delicious smoked ribs.

SMOKING ON YOUR GRILL

When you're ready to take on more than what is possible on your stove top, it's time to move your smoking outside and onto your grill. Using a grill allows you to smoke more meat, as well choose a meat that takes a longer time to cook. An extra bonus is that you don't have to worry about setting off your smoke alarm! This is a great method for smoking pork ribs, as well as fish, poultry, chops, steaks, and small roasts. Because the heat/smoke source and the meat are all in the same chamber, smoking on your grill is only suited for hot smoking.

ZONE GRILLING: SMOKING WITH INDIRECT HEAT

When it comes to grilling, you'll often hear people talk about direct heat, indirect heat, and zone grilling. "Direct heat" grilling refers to cooking something directly over the charcoal and/or flames. This is a hot and quick way of cooking best suited to steaks and chops. The temperature can easily get up to 600°F (315°C). With indirect heat, you're cooking the food without putting it in direct contact with the flame and/or charcoal. The way to manage this on a grill is to have the charcoal or wood only on one side of the grill, leaving the other half open. You can then place the food to be grilled on the side opposite from the charcoal — giving you an indirect heat zone on the grill (hence the term "zone grilling"). This allows you to cook the meat at lower temperatures for longer and, in general, gives you more control. You can still achieve a nice sear, if desired, by briefly moving the meat to the direct heat side.

One of the reasons I like smoking on a grill is that it is so accessible. A kettle grill allows you to smoke larger cuts, like a pork shoulder or a rack of ribs, without buying new equipment or investing your time in building a smoker. The drawback is that kettle grills are designed for grilling, which means that it can be challenging to maintain an even heat at a low temperature over a long period of time. And since kettle grills aren't very large, you'll be able to smoke a small pork shoulder, a whole chicken, a few pork chops, or one rack of ribs, but you aren't going to be able to feed your neighbors. While this technique for smoking is based on using a classic charcoal kettle grill, it can also be used with other kinds of grills, like a hibachi. The key is having a tight-fitting lid.

With "zone grilling," the fire is on one side of the grill and the meat is placed on the other side; this way, the meat can cook slowly at a lower temperature.

ALL ABOUT CHARCOAL

There are two kinds of charcoal available: lump and briquette.

Lump charcoal is made by charring logs of hardwood in a kiln. The shape and size of the pieces of charcoal are irregular. They look like what they are: chunks of charred wood. They can come in various types of hardwood including oak, mesquite, maple, or beech, or they can be labeled just as generic hardwood. Lump charcoal burns cleanly and starts out very hot. The temperature drops off pretty quickly after its initial burn, and the burn time in general is somewhat short, which means that for long cooking/smoking times, you will need to add more charcoal as you go. Since lump charcoal burns so cleanly, you can add it directly to your grill without creating an unpleasant-tasting smoke.

Briquettes are made from a combination of wood scraps, coal dust, and various chemical additives. These are those evenly shaped, square, black pillows you've seen. Unlike the lump charcoal, these burn at a consistent temperature for a long time, which is nice when you have a long cook/smoke time. The problem is that when the briquettes first burn, they give off a nasty-tasting smoke, because of the various chemical additives. If you decide to use briquettes, just remember that if you need to add more to your grill throughout your smoking, start the briquettes separately so your food doesn't get exposed to the bad-tasting smoke initially released from the briquettes.

Not surprisingly, I do not use briquettes. I am uncomfortable with the abundance of synthetic chemicals that are added to them. I'd rather deal with the somewhat irregular quality (in terms of shape, size, and temperature) and shorter burn time of lump charcoal than have lots of added chemicals in my fire and smoke. Also, I don't get that caught up in what kind of hardwood my lump charcoal is from; I tend to use generic hardwood lump charcoal.

LUMP CHARCOAL

BRIQUETTES

SMOKING ON A KETTLE GRILL

1. Fill a chimney starter with charcoal. Place a couple of fist-sized crumpled-up pieces of newspaper in the lower part of the chimney. Light the newspaper. Monitor the starter to make sure that the charcoal catches; if it doesn't catch right away, use more paper.

2. Once the charcoal has caught, let it burn for 10 to 15 minutes. Then the charcoal should be hot and gray and ready to use.

3. Once the charcoal is ready, pour it out of the starter into the grill, concentrating it to one side of the grill.

4. Place a mound of woodchips over the charcoal. Set the grill rack in place. Place the meat on the side of the grill rack where there is no charcoal and woodchips below.

5. Cover the grill and smoke the meat for the required amount of time (according to the recipe you're following). Monitor the grill temperature with a thermometer; depending on how long you're smoking, you may need to add more started charcoal and/or woodchips at some point in the process.

THE GRILL TABLE

Using a grill table is the most bare-bones way of smoking meat and the most reminiscent of the *barabicu* of the West Indies. This is still the preferred technique for smoking meats in most Asian and South American traditions. It is one of my favorite ways of smoking, and the one I rely on the most. I had a friend build me a grill table to my preferred specs, and I use it all the time. The grill table is one of my favorite cooking tools, and I would highly recommend building one or having one built for you. But you can also use almost anything. I have seen pictures of grill setups made from random grates (from old ovens, refrigerators, shelving units . . . you could use anything that's food safe) propped up on some rocks or cinder blocks. I like to have my grate a foot above the coals. I've even seen images of someone who built a fire under an old shopping cart and grilled in the cart.

Because you're doing this out in the open, you are not going to get the level of smokiness that you would in an enclosed space, like the kettle grill, or in the rest of the smokers. But with a properly managed fire, you do get a really nice, subtle smoke level on your meat. You also can't control the temperature very well with this method; a gust of wind can quickly change the fire, either feeding the flames or blowing them out. But with the right tools and experience, these issues become very manageable.

I like to use a grill table for pork ribs, chops, steaks, poultry, fish, and vegetables. I will often cook a large amount of sausages and burgers on my grill table to impart a wonderful smokiness on them. This same technique can be used for spit roasting a whole animal: just remove the grill from the setup and replace it with a spit. In Argentina they do something similar to spit roasting called *asador*. A whole animal (usually a lamb, goat, or pig) is butterflied and splayed on a large metal rod with two crosspieces. This cross is then placed at an angle over the coals to slowly roast the meat as it is infused with smoke. You then can add more charcoal as needed, or change the angle of the metal to bring the animal closer to

or farther away from the heat. It is a dramatic and fun way to feed a crowd.

One of the things I love about the grill table setup is that you can grill and smoke over it, and then when you're done cooking, you can move the grill off the firepit, throw more wood in, and get a big campfire going to stay warm by and watch the stars and fireflies. At our house, our grill table is the center of almost all activity from May through September.

SMOKING ON A GRILL TABLE

1. Build a fire, log cabin style. Start the fire at least 1 hour before you want to start smoking to ensure that you're cooking over hot coals and not flaming logs. To get a good bed of coals, build a large fire with split logs, four tiers high in a log cabin style (see page 50). The longer you want to smoke, the bigger the bed of coals you will need.

2. Rake the coals. Once your logs have burned down to a bed of hot coals, you're ready to get smoking. Rake the coals to create an even bed.

3. Keep feeding the coal bed. Keep a fire going with split logs to one side of the pit so that you can keep feeding the pit with hot coals. Be sure to keep whatever food you are grilling away from the direct flames of the burning split logs. Once you have an even bed of hot coals in your firepit, place your grill table over the coals. Now you're ready to cook.

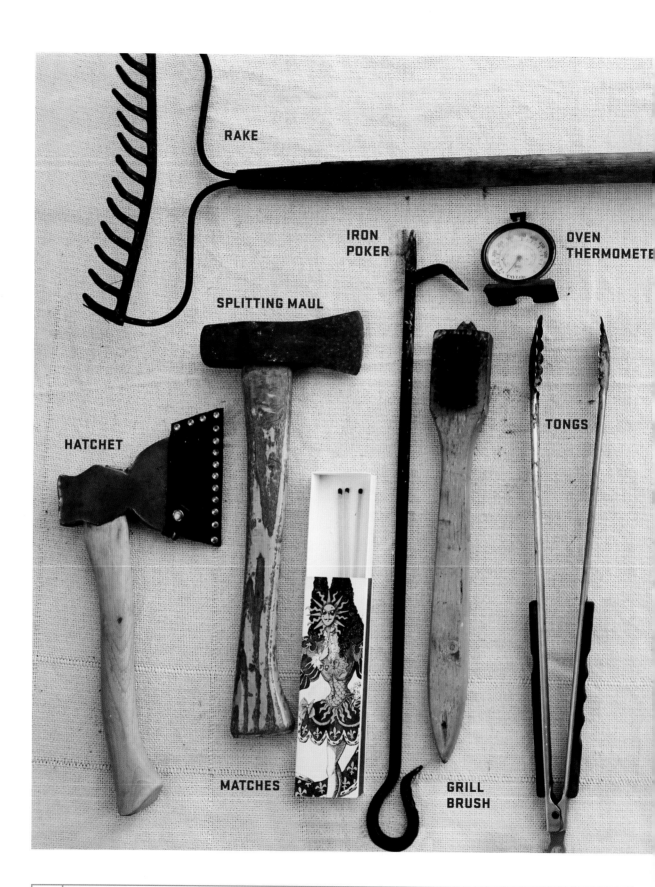

RAKE

IRON POKER

OVEN THERMOMETER

SPLITTING MAUL

HATCHET

TONGS

MATCHES

GRILL BRUSH

BACON HOOK

MEAT
THERMOMETERS

LEATHER WELDING GLOVES

TOOLS FOR SMOKING

Now that we've moved outside with our smoking and are getting a little more dirt on our hands, we should talk about some basic tools you'll want to have for any type of outdoor smoker. Most of these are common tools that you probably already have, but you might consider dedicating a separate set just to use with your smoker.

- A shovel with a wooden handle and metal head for digging as well as for moving hot coals

- A rake with a wooden handle and metal head for leveling your work area and for raking hot coals and pushing burning logs around

- A splitting maul for splitting logs

- A hatchet for cutting up kindling and tinder to start your fire

- A fire poker or blow poke for controlling your fire

- A grill brush for cleaning your grill

- Meats hooks, a bacon hook, and some smoke sticks (or lengths of rebar) for hanging bacon, sausages, and hams in your smokehouse

- Leather welding gloves to pick up burning hot metal and protecting your hands in general

- A charcoal chimney

- Long grill tongs with wooden handles

- A food-safe spray bottle

- A meat thermometer; a wireless meat thermometer that connects to a remote monitor is ideal, but an old-fashioned one works well, too

- An oven thermometer to monitor the temperature inside the smoker

- A good chef's knife or 8-inch scimitar/breaking knife

PIT SMOKING

Pit smoking is a very simple technique practiced throughout the world in its original form to this day. You can find it in Mexico, from the *cochinita pibil* of the Yucatán to goat *barbacoa* in Oaxaca. You'll also find it on the coast of Dakar, where miles of beach are scented by the smell of fish being smoked over grass in long open pits, and in New Zealand, where the Maori call it *hangi* and roast large root vegetables, lizards, and even whole emu.

Pit smoking is traditionally used for cooking whole animals — pigs, goats, and sheep are the most common — but it's also great for large cuts of meat. Beef *barbacoa*, a cowboy classic, traditionally uses a whole cow or steer's head. In most traditions, people dig a large pit in the ground and line it with stones, then make a large fire in order to build up a deep layer of hot coals. The meat and/or vegetables are often wrapped in some sort of organic material, such as large leaves, and placed on the coals. The pit is then covered and the food is buried. The deep layer of coals and the heat retained by the stones lining the pit slowly cook the food. Steam and smoke from the slowly burning organic matter help keep the food moist and flavorful. Often the food is left to cook all day or overnight. Because pit smoking is a long, slow cooking method, it's ideal for those tougher cuts with lots of collagen: heads, shoulders, and legs.

One of the benefits of cooking in a pit is that once you put your food in the pit, you don't have to fuss with it until it's ready. The downside is that you can't make adjustments; you can't open the pit to check the temperature or to add more fuel. The key to making this method work is having a deep enough bed of coals (1 to 2 feet deep); otherwise, your meat may not cook fully. (If this happens, simply serve the parts that are ready to eat and put the rest in the oven or on the grill.)

There are a lot of ways to build a pit for smoking, depending on how permanent you'd like the structure to be and how much time, money, and material you'd like to invest. Fortunately, you can always start with a simple, inexpensive, and temporary pit, then upgrade later if you decide you love pit smoking.

PIT SMOKING IN THE GROUND

1. Start a large fire in the pit. Build a large fire with split logs in your deep pit at least 4 hours before you want to start smoking. Not only do you want the stones and the pit to be hotter than hell, but you want to have a deep bed of coals, 12 to 24 inches deep. Unlike with a ground-level pit, you can't keep feeding the pit with new coals; once the meat has gone in and you've closed the pit, you just have to wait. If you don't build a deep enough bed of coals, you risk undercooking your meat.

2. Wrap the meat in an organic material. Besides being rubbed with a spice mix, traditionally the meat for pit smoking is wrapped in some sort of organic material like banana leaves, agave leaves, or corn husks. If you don't have access to any of those, you can use uncoated butcher's paper, craft paper, or burlap. Wrapping the meat helps protect it from getting burned, as it cooks directly on live coals. It also keeps the meat moist while it's cooking. Finally, it adds to the flavor; as the meat cooks, the heat also cooks the wrapping material, imparting a distinct flavor to the meat.

I love the smell of toasted banana leaves on the meat; they have a floral, tea-like aroma that I find intoxicating.

3. Rake the coals. You'll want to spread the coals out into an even bed.

4. Place the meat on the coals. Lower the wrapped meat and place directly on the bed of coals.

5. Cover the pit. Cover the pit with a piece of metal or a piece of plywood wrapped in aluminum foil. Cover the metal or plywood with about 6 inches of soil.

6. Smoke for several hours, then unearth. The cooking time depends on what you're cooking. A pork shoulder or brisket will take about 6 hours. A 75-pound pig will need about 9 hours. For every additional 25 pounds, add 3 hours of cooking time. Be sure to wear protective gear like leather gloves when removing something from the pit.

ABOVEGROUND PIT SMOKING

Another common version of pit smoking is essentially a combination of the techniques used for the grill table and the in-ground pit. It is aboveground, but enclosed. This style of pit is common in the American South (including at Salt Lick BBQ in Driftwood, Texas, shown below); it's also the technique that is employed along the coast of West Africa, where fish are smoked in long aboveground pits over millet grass. This type of pit is great for whole animals and large, tough cuts but can also be used for smaller, quicker items like fish and poultry.

VERTICAL SMOKERS

The 55-gallon drum barrel (or the manufactured smoker based on this simple design) has become a standard piece of equipment for backyard smoking enthusiasts, partly because 55-gallon drums are so ubiquitous. A quick search online will lead you to numerous forums dedicated to "ugly drum smokers" (UDS) and thousands of images of custom-designed smokers (some featuring people's favorite football teams, others designed to look like pigs, and so on). There are kits you can order online that supply you with all the hardware (other than the barrel) and instructions for building the smoker, and there are guides that require serious welding

chops and lots of power tools. The two simple designs in part 4 — one for hot smoking and one for cold smoking — don't require a metal shop.

OTHER OPTIONS FOR VERTICAL SMOKERS

The vertical smoker designs in part 4 call for a 55-gallon drum, but there are many alternatives: garbage cans, kegs, old oak whiskey barrels, and more. A popular option is an old filing cabinet: the upper drawers become smoke chambers where you place the meat, the second drawer from the bottom becomes the firebox, and the bottom drawer (with a few holes drilled in it) serves as the air intake and ash pan.

Old refrigerators can also be turned into this type of smoker. They're well insulated, so they hold temperature well, and they already have racks in them. Just be sure that the fridge is metal, not plastic. If you use an old refrigerator, rather than building a wood or charcoal fire directly in it, place an electric burner/plate in the bottom of the fridge, then place a metal roasting pan on the electric burner. Fill the roasting pan with woodchips or sawdust and turn the electric plate on. The heat from the plate should slowly burn the woodchips/sawdust, creating a nice smoke and consistent heat.

An offset smoker is essentially a drum smoker on its side.

SMOKING IN A **DRUM SMOKER**

1. Start some coals. Pour about a third of a bag of charcoal onto the lower grate. Using your chimney starter, start some additional charcoal. Once the charcoal has developed a coating of gray ash and is emanating heat, pour it over the unlit charcoal in the smoker.

2. Add chips. Pour in enough woodchips to cover the glowing coals.

3. Place the top grate over the coals and place the meat on the grate. Set the cooking grate in place and place your meat on the grate.

If you're smoking bacon or ribs, use a bacon hanger and hang them from the upper grate.

4. Cover with the lid and monitor the temperature. Once the meat is in the smoker, cover it with the lid and monitor the temperature, ideally keeping it between 200° and 250°F (95° and 120°C). You may have to add more woodchips or charcoal as you smoke, depending on how long you are smoking.

SMOKING IN A
COLD-SMOKE DRUM SMOKER

1. Put the meat in the smoker and cover the chamber. Place your cured meat onto, or hang it from, the grill grate in the smoking chamber. Cover the chamber with the lid.

2. Build the fire. In the firebox, build a fire using your desired hardwood. Once the fire has caught, close (or cover) the firebox.

3. Vent for air intake. To help feed the fire, you can slightly prop open the lid of the firebox using a stone or a stick. You may have to feed the fire depending on the desired smoke time.

OFF-THE-SHELF SMOKERS

Most smokers available at your local hardware store or from online retailers, including familiar models like the classic Weber Smokey Mountain smoker and other water or bullet smokers, are based on the design of the upright drum smoker. These industrially made models definitely come with some design advantages: it's easier to add charcoal or woodchips and to control the air intake and exhaust. Also, you don't have to spend time making your smoker. But what's the fun of that?

Offset drum smokers work on the same principle as the upright drum smoker and are just a little further up the evolutionary tree of hot-smoker designs. The real differences are that you have more rack space for meat (since the barrel is on its side rather than upright), and the fire is removed from the smoking chamber to a separate, offset chamber. The benefits to the offset smoker are that you can use split logs or charcoal, you have a bigger cooking chamber, and you have more control over temperature. The drawback is that they are heavy and awkward to move around. And in order to build one yourself, you need to have welding equipment and skills. If what

If you are more interested in smoking than in building a smoker, you might want to buy a commercial smoker. There are a lot of great options, including this standard offset smoker, which is great for barbecue, bacon, and hot smoked fish.

you are really interested in is barbecue, then this is great smoker for you.

Another commercially available option is Kamado cookers, such as the Big Green Egg, which, like offset smokers, have something of a cult following. These ceramic cookers combine the design principles of a kettle grill and a pit. As with the upright barrel, you use a combination of charcoal and woodchips as your fuel, placing the food above the fuel source to catch the heat and smoke. Like a pit, the ceramic cooker maintains a consistent heat for a long period of time, because the thick ceramic-lined walls hold the heat generated by the fire. These cookers have wonderful temperature and airflow control. They're also versatile, allowing you to cook something for a long period of time at a low temperature or quickly with very high heat. As with a kettle grill, though, you don't have much space to cook on. They're also difficult to reload with fuel in the middle of cooking (though you're not likely to need to reload, since they hold temperature so well). They are also very heavy and can be somewhat fragile, because they are ceramic, and they tend to be very expensive.

Combining the design principles of a kettle grill with a pit, ceramic cookers like the Big Green Egg maintain a consistent temperature for a long time.

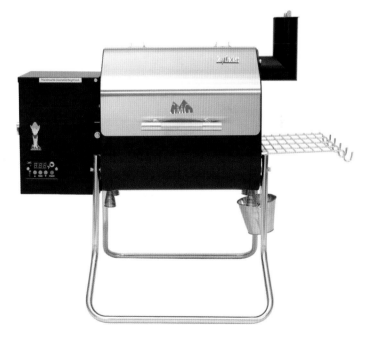

Portable pellet smokers offer versatility and greater temperature control. The Davy Crockett from Green Mountain Grills, shown, can be controlled via WI-FI connection.

My tri-purpose smokehouse, named Frazier, was a team effort: I brought the experience with smoking techniques, and my brother Will contributed his building expertise. Made out of cob and wood with a firebrick-lined pit connected via stovepipe, it allows me to hot smoke, cold smoke, and pit roast.

THE SMOKEHOUSE

If at this point you have tried some of the smaller smokers and still want more — more space, more versatility, more permanence — then you are probably ready to build a smokehouse. This is a permanent structure that takes a fair amount of time and materials to build, as well as a familiarity with building techniques and masonry. It is a commitment, but it is a commitment that pays it back. A century ago, some variation or another of this type of smokehouse could be found on almost every farm. The one that was on my grandfather's farm in the East End of Long Island, which we called Harriet, is now, sadly, a tool shed.

I've designed what I call a tri-purpose smokehouse (see page 168) — if you build it with cob or another masonry material and build it with a full-size firepit, you can smoke using three different techniques. By building a fire in the pit and hanging meat in the smokehouse, you can cold smoke. By building a fire directly in the smokehouse and hanging the meat above it, you can hot smoke. By building a fire in the pit and building up a deep coal bed, you can pit roast in the pit. We love having one structure that can smoke all three ways; we've even pit roasted and cold smoked at the same time.

A SMOKEHOUSE MADE OF WOOD

You could make your smokehouse out of wood; you just won't be able to hot smoke in it. Many of the old farmhouse and homestead smokehouses were made from wood and were dedicated to cold smoking. My friend Dominic Palumbo built a wooden smokehouse on his farm — Moon in the Pond Farm in Sheffield, Massachusetts — more than 20 years ago. He still uses it regularly, cold smoking hundreds of pounds of pork every year.

PIT ROASTING IN A
TRI-PURPOSE SMOKEHOUSE

1. Start a fire in the pit. At least 4 hours before you want to start smoking, build a large fire with split logs in the pit. You want the bricks and the pit to be very hot, and there should be a 12- to 24-inch-deep bed of coals.

2. Wrap the meat. Traditionally the meat for pit roasting is wrapped in banana leaves, agave leaves, corn husks, or another organic material. Alternatively, you could use uncoated butcher paper, craft paper, or burlap. Wrapping the meat helps protect it from getting burned, as it cooks directly on live coals, and keeps the meat moist. The aroma of the smoldering wrapping material also imparts a distinct flavor to the meat.

3. Rake the coals and place the meat. The coals should be spread into an even bed. Lower the wrapped meat directly onto the bed of coals.

4. Cover the pit. Cover the pit with a piece of metal or a piece of plywood wrapped in aluminum foil. Cover the metal or plywood with about 6 inches of soil.

5. Smoke for several hours, then unearth. The cooking time depends on what you're cooking. A pork shoulder or brisket will take about 6 hours. A 75-pound pig will need about 9 hours. For every additional 25 pounds, add 3 hours of cooking time. Be sure to wear protective gear like leather gloves when removing the meat from the pit.

HOT SMOKING IN THE SMOKEHOUSE

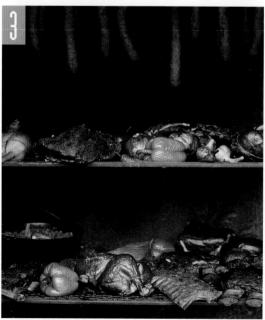

1. Start the fire. Build a fire using split logs in a log cabin style (see page 50) on the bottom of the smoke chamber of the smokehouse.

2. Bring the smokehouse to temperature. Keep the fire going, monitoring the temperature within the smokehouse. I like to use an old-fashioned oven thermometer for this, but you can also use a digital thermometer. (This is where a remote digital thermometer can come in handy — especially a dual-probe digital remote thermometer designed for grilling and barbecuing.)

3. Put the meat in smoker. Place the meat on the middle and upper racks in your chamber. Be sure you are monitoring the temperature on the racks where you are placing the meat; different racks will have different temperatures. Close the door and monitor the temperature, ideally keeping it between 200° and 250°F (95° and 120°C), depending on what you are smoking. You may have to add more logs as you smoke, depending on how long you are smoking for.

COLD SMOKING IN THE SMOKEHOUSE

1. Place the meat in the smokehouse and close the door. Place your cured meat on one of the lower shelves or hang in the smoking chamber.

2. Build the fire. In the firebox, build a fire using your desired hardwood. Once the fire has caught, close (or cover) the firebox. You may have to refeed the fire depending on the desired smoke time.

PART 3

RECIPES

There are thousands of different recipes, techniques, and flavor profiles you can employ when smoking food. In this section, I've included what I consider to be classic recipes and basic techniques, along with some alternatives — ways of combining less common flavor profiles with different techniques. It's a sort of remixing of cultures and traditions. There are recipes for hot smoking and recipes for cold smoking. There are some that are better suited for the grill table, and others better suited for the smokehouse or the vertical hot smoker. These recipes come from my years of experimenting and playing; my goal is to provide you with a framework you can play with, so that you can experiment and invent your own recipes.

HOT-SMOKING RECIPES

These recipes cover what I consider the classics of hot smoking and offer some alternatives for each of those classics, including American barbecue, bacon, sausage, and hams. I also include some hot-smoking recipes that are a little less standard but are some of my personal favorites.

RUBS

It seems like a lot of people who are interested in hot smoking are really interested in American barbecue. And the first step in any good barbecue is a good rub. Not only does it help to create a nice pellicle, but it adds to the flavor and color of the meat.

My basic rub is simply ½ cup of salt mixed with ½ cup of black pepper. I keep this mixture on hand at all times, and whenever I'm getting ready to smoke some ribs, a pork shoulder, a brisket, or some beef ribs, I grab a handful and add some other ground spices, depending on what mood I'm in: ground ancho chile, ground chipotle, onion powder, smoked paprika, cumin, coriander, mace, or ground coffee, for example. When adding other spices and herbs, I make sure that the total amount of these other seasonings doesn't add up to more than half of the amount of pepper.

When I veer away from my standard rubs, I use classic spice combinations established by culinary tradition as my starting point. I start

with something like the Spanish combination of smoked paprika and garlic; the English combination of sage, coriander, nutmeg, and mace; the Sichuan combination of star anise, cinnamon, clove, ginger, fennel, and Sichuan pepper; or the Mexican combination of cumin, coriander, garlic, and cayenne. If I am feeling unsure of ratios or exact spice combinations, I turn to a favorite recipe and extrapolate from there. Below are a few examples of some variations I have come up with, but I encourage you to explore and create your own. In general, a tablespoon of rub is enough for 1 pound of meat.

PORK BARBECUE RUB

Makes about 1¾ cups

This rub is perfect for barbecued ribs and pork shoulders. It also works well as a generic taco seasoning.

½ cup fine sea salt or kosher salt	2 tablespoons ground coriander
½ cup ground black pepper	2 tablespoons ground cumin
¼ cup muscovado sugar	1 tablespoon garlic powder
3 tablespoons sweet paprika	1 teaspoon ground cayenne pepper

Mix the ingredients together and store in an airtight container in a cool, dry place.

"CHAR SIU" RUB

Makes about 1½ cups

Char siu — which I've tried to emulate with this rub — is the Chinese counterpart to American barbecue. Like American barbecue, it combines sweet and spicy with strong aromatics. As I smoke the meat, I periodically glaze it with a sauce made up of hoisin sauce, garlic, honey, and soy sauce. Use this rub on any meat, but especially pork and poultry.

½ cup fine sea salt or kosher salt	1 tablespoon ground cinnamon
¼ cup muscovado sugar	1 tablespoon ground fennel
3 tablespoons garlic powder	1 tablespoon ground ginger
3 tablespoons ground Sichuan pepper	1 tablespoon ground star anise
3 tablespoons sweet paprika	1 teaspoon ground cloves

Mix the ingredients together and store in an airtight container in a cool, dry place.

THAI RUB

Makes about 1½ cups

This recipe was inspired by an Andy Ricker recipe for pork ribs from his book *Pok Pok.* In my mind, there is no question that his recipe with fresh and wet ingredients mixed with a mortar and pestle is better than mine, but it's also a lot of work — and it's challenging to source all of the ingredients. So this is a bit of a shortcut. As you smoke the ribs, try glazing them with a sauce of honey, soy sauce, and Shaoxing wine.

½ cup fine sea salt or kosher salt	1 tablespoon garlic powder
¼ cup ground white pepper	1 tablespoon ground ginger
¼ cup palm sugar or light brown sugar, lightly packed	1 tablespoon ground Thai chiles
3 tablespoons ground coriander	1 teaspoon ground cinnamon
2 tablespoons ground cumin	½ teaspoon ground nutmeg

Mix the ingredients together and store in an airtight container in a cool, dry place.

BEEF BARBECUE RUB

Makes about 1⅓ cups

For beef barbecue, I prefer a simpler rub. I also leave out the sugar because it tends to burn a little over the longer cook time required for most beef barbecue. And, in general, I don't like my beef as sweet as my pork barbecue.

½ cup fine sea salt or kosher salt	1 tablespoon garlic powder
½ cup ground black pepper	1 tablespoon onion powder
3 tablespoons sweet paprika	1 teaspoon ground cayenne pepper

Mix the ingredients together and store in an airtight container in a cool, dry place.

A WORD ABOUT UNITS OF MEASUREMENT

You'll notice that some of the recipes in this book include imperial and metric measures, as well as percentages. In the meat-curing world, we rely on weight as our preferred measurement in recipes. The reason to use weight rather than volume, which is often used in American recipes, is because it is more consistent. One pound of salt is a pound of salt no matter what. But 1 cup of salt may have a different weight depending on the kind or brand of salt. Or think of the classic recipe instruction for 1 cup of packed brown sugar. Depending on who is packing it and what brand is being used, that cup may weigh ½ pound or it may weigh 1 pound. Using volume as a unit of measurement creates inconsistencies in recipes in a way that weight rarely can.

In addition to measuring by weight rather than volume, it's helpful to use metric measurements. The metric system is based on units of 10, which allows us to easily scale a recipe up or down. This is important because the weights of cuts of meat can vary greatly. Some bellies may be 10 pounds, while others might weigh 15 pounds, depending on how they were cut and how big the animal was.

Scaling up or down with metric measurements is far easier than with imperial. For instance, if you had a piece of meat that was 5 kilograms and the cure required adding 3 percent salt, you could do that math in your head and figure out that you need 150 grams of salt. Now let's try that in imperial: You have a 10-pound piece of meat and you need 3 percent salt. Since the smaller increment of pounds is ounces, it's easier to first convert the pounds to ounces; in this case it would be 160 ounces. Now we need to find 3 percent of 160 ounces by multiplying it by 0.03, which gets us . . . 4.8 ounces. It's still possible to calculate, just not as simple.

Having the right percentage of salt and curing salt is crucial for many recipes — not only for flavor, but also for food safety. For recipes where precision is less important, I stick to the standard imperial system and volumes. No matter which units you go by, I strongly recommend that you purchase a good kitchen scale that measures in both imperial and metric units.

BRINES

The purpose of brining meat is to simultaneously introduce salt and moisture into it. Brining is essential for producing moist, delicious smoked poultry, as well as for making smoked hams for your holiday dinner or sandwich meat.

I generally start with my basic brine and then — depending on what kind of meat I'm brining and what flavors I'm looking for — adjust from there. Some meats, like pork, can take more salt than, say, poultry. Sometimes I'm just interested in adding salt and moisture; other times I use my brine as a way of pumping the meat full of other flavors, like ginger, apple cider, and star anise. When you decide you want to start to experiment with your own brine recipes, it's always good to start with a classic flavor profile or spice and aromatic combination.

BASIC BRINE

Makes about 4 quarts

For just about any type or cut of meat, this brine will provide you with the right amount of saltiness (at a salinity of 6.25 percent) and sweetness without overpowering the flavor of the meat. While I often tweak my brines to meet the needs of what I'm cooking, this brine is the base brine from which I build all other brines. Sometimes I'll use cider instead of water; add fresh ginger and star anise; throw in bay leaves, black pepper, and juniper; substitute the sugar with honey or maple syrup; include a huge bouquet of various fresh herbs; or put in a head of garlic and a large yellow onion. The possibilities are endless! This recipe provides enough brine for one whole chicken or six pork chops.

4   quarts/4 liters water

¾   cup/250 grams fine sea salt
    or kosher salt

½   cup/150 grams sugar

Combine all of the ingredients in a large pot and bring to a simmer, stirring to dissolve the salt and sugar. Remove from the heat and allow to cool to room temperature. Refrigerate until chilled.

BRINED AND SMOKED CHICKEN

Chicken was one of the first meats I experimented with smoking at home. It is a project you can do relatively easily in a stove-top smoker (as long as you have a good kitchen fan), it doesn't require hours and hours of smoking, and if you mess up (which I certainly did the first few times) you won't go bankrupt. This is my standard poultry brine, whether I'm smoking a chicken or turkey (or even rabbit) or making fried chicken. It is wonderfully herbal and bright but doesn't mask the flavor of the meat. Smoking poultry is perfect for a kettle grill smoker, a hot-smoke drum smoker, an aboveground pit, or your smokehouse (if it's built for hot smoking).

Serves 2 to 4 people

- 4 quarts/4 liters water
- ⅔ cup/225 grams fine sea salt or kosher salt
- ¼ cup/75 grams sugar, honey, or maple syrup
- 12 bay leaves
- 1 head garlic, smashed but not peeled
- 1 medium yellow onion, halved but not peeled
- 2 tablespoons black peppercorns
- 3 large rosemary sprigs
- 1 small bunch parsley
- 1 small bunch sage
- 1 small bunch thyme
- 3 lemons, halved
- 1 3- to 5-pound/1.4- to 2.3-kilogram chicken

1. Combine the water, salt, sugar, bay leaves, garlic, onion, peppercorns, rosemary, parsley, sage, thyme, and lemons in a large nonreactive pot and bring to a boil. Stir until the salt and sugar are completely dissolved. Remove from the heat and let cool completely.

2. Submerge the chicken completely in the brine solution (you may need to weigh it down), and refrigerate overnight (at least 8 hours but no more than 12 hours).

3. Remove the chicken from the brine, rinse under cold water, pat dry, and let air-dry, uncovered, on a wire rack on a sheet pan in your fridge for at least a few hours, and ideally overnight.

4. Hot smoke the poultry at 200° to 250°F (95° to 120°C) until the thigh reaches an internal temperature of 165°F (74°C), 3 to 5 hours. Allow to cool for 10 minutes, then serve.

SMOKED THANKSGIVING TURKEY

With the completion of our very own backyard smoke-house came a new Thanksgiving tradition: smoked turkey. Now I always smoke one bird and roast another. (I keep saying one of these years I will do a third bird, either on the grill or in a fryer.) Whether roasted or smoked, I like to brine both birds. With the one we roast, I experiment with the brines a bit to see what new flavors I can introduce to the holiday table, but what I've included below is my standard Thanksgiving smoked turkey brine. This recipe plays off traditional autumnal flavors, while still bringing a brightness to the meat. If you don't have a smokehouse (yet!), you can smoke the turkey on a kettle grill, on a drum smoker, or in an aboveground pit.

Serves 10 to 15 people

- 4 quarts/4 liters water
- 4 quarts/4 liters apple cider
- 1⅓ cups/450 grams fine sea salt or kosher salt
- ½ cup/150 grams sugar, honey, or maple syrup
- 12 bay leaves
- 2 heads garlic, smashed but not peeled
- 2 medium yellow onions, halved but not peeled
- 2 4-inch pieces fresh ginger, cut into 1-inch lengths
- ¼ cup/30 grams black peppercorns
- 1 large bunch parsley
- 1 large bunch rosemary sprigs
- 1 large bunch sage
- 1 large bunch thyme
- 6 lemons, halved
- 1 10- to 15-pound/4.5- to 6.8-kilogram turkey

1. Combine the water, apple cider, salt, sugar, bay leaves, garlic, onions, ginger, peppercorns, parsley, rosemary, sage, thyme, and lemons in a large pot and bring to a boil. Stir until the salt and sugar are completely dissolved. Remove from the heat and let cool completely.

2. Submerge the turkey completely in the brine solution (you may need to weigh the turkey down) in a nonreactive container, and refrigerate for 24 hours.

3. Remove the turkey from the brine, rinse under cold water, pat dry, and let it air-dry, uncovered, on a wire rack set on a sheet pan in your fridge overnight to allow the surface to dry out and develop a pellicle.

4. Hot smoke the turkey between 225° and 275°F (110° and 135°C), until the thigh reaches an internal temperature of 165°F (74°C), 5 to 8 hours. Allow to cool for 10 minutes, then serve.

CANADIAN BACON

Canadian bacon is a wonderful alternative to traditional American bacon. It is a leaner bacon because it comes from the loin rather than the belly (like traditional English bacons). Because the loin is so much leaner than belly, Canadian bacon is brined so that it remains juicy when it is smoked and then fried. I like my Canadian bacon to be simple, on the sweeter side, and reflective of the flavor of Canada's greatest food product: maple syrup!

Serves 14 people

- 4 quarts/4 liters water
- 1 cup/300 grams fine sea salt or kosher salt
- 1½ cups/300 grams maple syrup
  Cure #1 or Veg Stable 504 salt (use supplier's recommended quantity)
- 1 4-pound/2-kilogram pork loin, skin off, bone out, with a ¼-inch fat cap on it

1. Combine the water with the sea salt, maple syrup, and curing salt in a saucepan and bring to a boil. Stir until the salt and sugar are completely dissolved. Remove from the heat and allow to cool completely.

2. Submerge the loin in a nonreactive container in the cooled brine and weight it down so that it remains completely covered by the brine. Brine in the refrigerator for 1 day for every 2 pounds (1 kilogram), or 2 days total.

3. After the allotted time, remove the loin from the brine, rinse under cool water, and pat dry. Place on a wire rack set on a sheet pan and refrigerate, uncovered, overnight to allow the surface to dry out and develop a pellicle.

4. Hot smoke the loin, ideally between 200° and 225°F (95° and 110°C), until the internal temperature reaches 150°F (65°C). Remove the meat from the smoker and allow to cool for 30 minutes, and then refrigerate for up to 10 days or freeze.

5. When you are ready to cook some Canadian bacon, slice thinly and fry in a pan like you would traditional bacon.

HOLIDAY HAM (AND HOCKS)

This is the recipe I used for our first Christmakkah ham, when I (sort of) smoked it in our oven. I still use this brine for our Christmas ham every year, only now I smoke it in our smokehouse — much better than trying to smoke in a city apartment oven. The flavor this brine brings to your ham (or hocks) is very traditional. The ciders help to sweeten it and the cloves add that classic holiday ham flavor. If you have a smaller ham, you can smoke this on your kettle grill; you can also use a hot-smoke drum smoker or an aboveground pit.

Serves 15 people

- 2 quarts/2 liters water
- 1 cup/300 grams fine sea salt or kosher salt
- 1½ cups/300 grams dark brown sugar or maple sugar
- Cure #1 or Veg Stable 504 salt (use supplier's recommended quantity)
- ¼ cup/30 grams black peppercorns
- 10 bay leaves
- 10 cloves
- 1 quart/1 liter fresh cider
- 1 quart/1 liter dry hard cider
- 1 12- to 15-pound/5.5- to 7-kilogram fresh ham, skin off, bone in or out, or 8 fresh ham hocks (about 1 pound/ 0.5 kilogram each)

1. Combine the water with the sea salt, brown sugar, curing salt, peppercorns, bay leaves, and cloves in a saucepan and bring to a boil. Stir until the salt and sugar are completely dissolved. Remove from the heat immediately and stir in with fresh and dry hard ciders. Allow to cool completely.

2. Submerge the ham in a nonreactive container in the cooled brine and weight it down so that it remains completely covered by the brine. Brine in the refrigerator for 1 day for every 2 pounds (1 kilogram), or 6 to 8 days total. If you're brining a bone-in ham, it is a good precaution to use a brine injector. (See page 29 for more information on using a brine injector.)

3. After the allotted time, remove the ham from the brine, rinse under cool water, and pat dry. Place on a wire rack set on a sheet pan and refrigerate, uncovered, overnight to allow the surface to dry out and develop a pellicle.

4. Hot smoke the ham, ideally between 200° and 225°F (95° and 110°C), until the internal temperature reaches 150°F (65°C). Remove the meat from the smoker and allow to cool for 30 minutes; then serve or refrigerate.

BRITISH BRINE

Another style of brine that I have come to love is inspired by traditional British brines for hams and back bacon (loin with some of the belly still attached). This recipe plays off bitter flavors rather than the sweet ones, using ingredients like blackstrap molasses, bitter ale, juniper, and bay leaves. This produces a great ham that is less sweet and has a more complex flavor than holiday ham (page 99). It also works nicely for bacon, back bacon, a turkey, or a leg of lamb. If you have a small ham (or turkey or leg of lamb), you can smoke it on your kettle grill. If you are smoking a large ham (or belly, back bacon, turkey, or leg of lamb), it will work best in a hot-smoke drum smoker or smokehouse.

1. Combine 2 quarts of the water with the sea salt, molasses, curing salt, juniper berries, peppercorns, bay leaves, and cloves in a saucepan and bring to a boil, stirring until the salt dissolves. Remove from the heat immediately and combine with the ale. Allow to cool completely.

2. In a nonreactive container, submerge the meat in the cooled brine and weight it down so that it remains completely covered by brine. Brine in the refrigerator for 1 day for every 2 pounds (1 kilogram), or 6 to 8 days total. If you're brining a bone-in ham or leg of lamb, it is a good precaution to use a brine injector. (See page 29 for more information about using a brine injector.)

3. After the allotted time, remove the meat from the brine, rinse under cool water, and pat dry. Place on a rack on a sheet pan and refrigerate, uncovered, overnight to allow the surface to dry out and develop a pellicle.

4. With this recipe you can either hot smoke or cold smoke. To hot smoke, smoke at a temperature between 200° and 225°F (95° and 110°C) until the meat reaches an internal temperature of 150°F (65°C). Remove from the smoker and allow to cool for 30 minutes, then serve or refrigerate. To cold smoke, place the meat in cold smoker and smoke for 6 to 24 hours, depending on how strong of a smoke flavor you want.

Serves 10 people

- 2 quarts/2 liters water
- 1 cup/300 grams fine sea salt or kosher salt
- 1 cup/300 grams blackstrap molasses

  Cure #1 or Veg Stable 504 (use supplier's recommended quantity)
- 20–30 juniper berries
- ¼ cup/30 grams black peppercorns
- 10 bay leaves
- 10 cloves
- 1 quart/1 liter bitter ale, such as an India pale ale (IPA) or extra special bitter (ESB)
- 1 7- to 15-pound/ 3- to 7-kilogram piece of meat (fresh ham, pork loin, leg of lamb, or whole turkey are best)

SHAMB (LAMB, MUTTON, OR GOAT HAM)

When I was a butcher at *The Meat Market in Great Barrington, Massachusetts,* one of my favorite recipes we developed was for a leg of mutton that was brined, smoked, and treated like traditional American ham. In thinking about our brine, we wanted to keep it simple so the flavor of the mutton would be the highlight. We included the bay leaves and juniper to bring some of that classic Alpine flavor that goes so well with mutton. We dubbed it a "shamb." If you have a small ham, you can smoke it on your kettle grill, but I prefer to do it in a hot-smoke drum smoker or smokehouse.

Serves 10 people

- 4 quarts/4 liters water
- 1 cup/300 grams fine sea salt or kosher salt
- ⅓ cup/100 grams sugar
  Cure #1 or Veg Stable 504 (use supplier's recommended quantity)
- 1 tablespoon crushed juniper berries
- 3 bay leaves
- 1 7- to 10-pound/3- to 4.5-kilogram leg of lamb, mutton, or goat (bone in or out)

1. To make the brine, combine the water with the sea salt, sugar, curing salt, juniper berries, and bay leaves in a saucepan and bring to a boil, stirring until the sugar and salt completely dissolve. Remove from the heat immediately and allow to cool completely.

2. In a nonreactive container, submerge the meat in the brine and weight it down so that it remains completely covered by the brine. Brine for 1 day for every 2 pounds (1 kilogram), or 4 to 5 days. If you are brining a bone-in leg, it is a good precaution to use a brine injector. (See page 29 for information on using a brine injector.)

3. After the allotted time, remove the meat from the brine, rinse under cool water, and pat dry. Place on a rack on a sheet pan and refrigerate, uncovered, overnight to allow the surface to dry out and develop a pellicle.

4. Hot smoke the meat, ideally between 200° and 225°F (95° and 110°C), until the meat reaches an internal temperature of 150°F (66°C). Remove from the smoker and allow to cool for 30 minutes, then serve or refrigerate.

THE STORY OF SHAMB

At the Meat Market, I was lucky to work with some amazing people and farms. One of these was Kinderhook Farm in Kinderhook, New York, which has an exceptional lamb program led by their shepherd, Anna Hodson. The farmers at Kinderhook were starting to experiment with keeping their lambs for a longer period of time and raising hogget (a sheep that is between 1 and 2 years old) and mutton (a sheep that is older than 2 years), and they asked us at the Meat Market if we would work with them to evaluate their meat quality. This was an exciting opportunity for us. Jamie Paxton, the chef at the Meat Market, and I were particularly interested in what kind of value-added products we could make. "Shamb" — a leg of mutton treated like ham — was one of the most delicious results of our partnership.

PASTRAMI

When I was growing up, going to New York City to visit my grandparents was always an exciting event filled with epicurean treats. I particularly enjoyed staying at my grandmother's apartment in midtown Manhattan, because that meant I would get to visit one of my favorite restaurants in all of New York City — the famed Carnegie Deli. The menu was filled with the foods of my family's people, eastern European Jews who had landed in New York City between the late 1800s and early 1900s. While there were tons of items on the menu, I had eyes for only one: a pastrami sandwich on rye piled high with thinly sliced, glistening pastrami and coated in a thick slathering of grainy mustard. This version of pastrami can be smoked in a kettle grill, hot-smoke drum smoker, or smokehouse (if it's built for hot smoking).

1. To make the brine, combine the water with the sea salt, brown sugar, curing salt, peppercorns, mustard seeds, juniper berries, coriander seeds, bay leaves, and garlic in a saucepan and bring to a boil, stirring until the salt and brown sugar completely dissolve. Remove from the heat immediately and allow to cool completely.

2. In a nonreactive container, submerge the brisket in the brine and weight it down so that it remains completely covered by the brine. Brine for at least 7 days but no more than 10 days.

3. After the allotted time, remove the brisket from the brine, rinse under cool water, and pat dry.

4. Make the rub by combining the black pepper, coriander, brown sugar, garlic powder, onion powder, and mustard powder. Coat the entire brisket in the rub. Place the meat on a rack on a sheet pan and refrigerate, uncovered, overnight to allow the surface to dry out and develop a pellicle.

5. Hot smoke the brisket, ideally between 200° and 225°F (95° and 110°C), until the internal temperature reaches 150°F (65°C), 4 to 6 hours. Remove from the smoker and allow to cool. Refrigerate overnight.

6. Bring a large pot of water to a boil. Place the pastrami in a steam basket or a bamboo steamer that fits in the pot. Place the steam basket over the boiling water. Steam the pastrami for about 2 hours, until a fork can be inserted easily into the meat, but the meat is not completely falling apart. Add water to the pot as needed.

7. Slice the pastrami against the grain and serve hot with rye bread, spicy mustard, and pickles.

BRINE

4 quarts/4 liters water

¾ cup/225 grams fine sea salt or kosher salt

½ cup/150 grams dark brown sugar, firmly packed

Cure #1 or Veg Stable 504 (use supplier's recommended quantity)

2 tablespoons black peppercorns

1 tablespoon yellow mustard seeds

1 tablespoon crushed juniper berries

3 tablespoons coriander seeds

5 bay leaves

1 head garlic, smashed but not peeled

RUB

¾ cup ground black pepper

¾ cup ground coriander

3 tablespoons dark brown sugar

1 tablespoon garlic powder

1 tablespoon onion powder

2 teaspoons mustard powder

1 3- to 5-pound/1.3- to 2.25-kilogram brisket, with fat cap

QUICK-SMOKED FOODS

Smoking doesn't always have to be a long, laborious process. There are many great, quick, and simple ways of producing smoked food. Sometimes I'll come home after a long day of work, grab a beer, get my Weber kettle grill going, put a handful of woodchips on the charcoal, and throw on some pork chops (or a steak) and 15 minutes later I have delicious smoked meat for dinner. Seafood is another great option when you're looking for a quick smoked meal. Here are a few of my favorite smoked recipes for weeknight dinners.

SMOKED BLUEFISH

I will never be able to replicate the first smoked mackerel I ever had (see My Mackerel Memory, page 108), but that doesn't stop me from trying. This recipe works equally well with mackerel, trout, or salmon. It's perfect for stove-top smoking but also works beautifully on a kettle grill, on a grill table, or in a hot-smoke drum smoker.

Serves 2 to 4 people

- 2 large bluefish or mackerel, weighing about 2 pounds each, scaled, filleted, and pin bones removed
- ½ cup fine sea salt or kosher salt
- ¼ cup ground black pepper

1. Lay the fish fillets out on your cutting board and sprinkle them with the salt, about 2 tablespoons per fillet. Let rest for 15 to 25 minutes. Then wash the salt off the fillets under cold water and pat dry. Sprinkle 1 tablespoon of ground pepper over each fillet, evenly coating them.

2. Place the fish in the smoker, skin side down, and smoke at 175°F (135°C) for about 20 minutes, until the fish is just cooked through but still moist. (If you are smoking mackerel or trout, smoke for 10 minutes.)

3. Serve right away or refrigerate. I love smoked fish when it is served cold with some bread and butter or mayo.

MUSSELS SMOKED IN PINE NEEDLES

*Every summer we spend a week at my grandparents'
farm on the eastern tip of Long Island. We are extremely
lucky because the farm is about a quarter-mile walk from
the beach. Our time out there is never complete without
a beach picnic, much of it cooked over a campfire.
Recently, I added another component to our beach-
picnic repertoire — mussels smoked in pine needles. This
is a show-stopping party trick that couldn't be easier to
pull off. The smoky, resiny aroma of pine needles is the
perfect balance to the sweet, briny flavor of the mussels.*

Serves 4 people

2 pounds mussels,
scrubbed and debearded

1. Place the mussels in the
sand (or on a sheet pan or
large smooth stone) hinge
side down. It is best to group
them in a circular formation.
If you are having a hard time
balancing them so they stay
upright, use another stone in
the center of the formation to
prop the mussels up against.

2. Completely cover the mussels with a 6-inch-thick layer
of dried pine needles.

3. Light the needles on fire
either with a match/lighter or
by placing a burning coal on
them. Let the needles completely burn out, about 5 minutes or so. The mussels should
have opened up and are ready
to eat.

MY MACKEREL MEMORY

My first time eating smoked mackerel is one of those Proustian memories: It was Father's Day, and we were in Cornwall, England, for a family trip. The village we were staying in had one of those classic, large, white plastered buildings with a big smokestack, right on the water's edge. My brother and I decided that buying our dad some smoked mackerel would be the perfect Father's Day present — one that we would benefit from. I can remember that first bite so vividly. The mackerel was still warm from the smoker, and the oak smoke balanced perfectly with the briny oil of the fish, with the delicate flesh flaking apart and melting in my mouth. When people ask me about my love of smoked food, this memory looms large.

TEA-SMOKED DUCK BREAST

This recipe is quick and easy but can also be a real crowd pleaser. My wife and I are just as likely to make it for the two of us as we are to make it for a large group as part of a Sichuan feast. While the flavor benefits from the meat having a longer cure time (overnight), we have been known to decide the morning of to defrost some breasts and have tea-smoked duck for dinner the same night. The marinade brightens up the flavor of the duck breast, while the earthy, floral aroma from the tea and rice adds an unexpected complexity to it, without being overpowering. This is perfect for a stove-top smoker, but you can also do it on a kettle grill.

Serves 2 to 4 people

- 2 ¾- to 1-pound boneless duck breasts
- 2 tablespoons fine sea salt or kosher salt
- 2 tablespoons ground Sichuan pepper
- 2 tablespoons Shaoxing wine
- ½ cup long-grain white rice
- ½ cup loose black tea, such as Ceylon, Darjeeling, and/or jasmine
- ½ cup dark brown sugar, firmly packed
- 1 star anise
- 4 4-inch sticks cinnamon

1. Score the skin of the duck breasts, without cutting the flesh, in a crosshatch pattern. Coat the duck breasts in the salt and Sichuan pepper, place in a nonreactive container or plastic bag, and pour in the wine. Let cure a minimum of 2 hours, and ideally overnight.

2. Remove the duck breasts from the cure, rinse under cool water, and pat dry.

3. Mix together the rice, loose tea, brown sugar, star anise, and cinnamon. Line the bottom of your stove-top smoker pan with aluminum foil. Pour in the tea mixture. Level it out into an even layer.

4. Place the duck breasts, skin side up, on a rack over the tea mixture. Place the pan over high heat. Once the mixture starts to smoke, cover the setup and turn the heat down to medium-low. Smoke the duck breasts for 20 minutes.

5. Preheat a cast-iron pan over high heat. Remove the duck breasts from the smoker and place them in the pan, skin side down. Sear the duck breasts until the skin is crispy and golden brown; it should only take a couple of minutes.

6. Let rest for 10 minutes; the duck can be served at room temperature or cold.

BARBECUE

When most Americans hear "smoked food," they think of barbecue, and for good reason. Whether it's from North Carolina or west Texas or somewhere in between, American barbecue is one of my favorite kinds of cooking. If I had to pick a type of food or dish that most represented the United States, I would choose barbecue without hesitation. Barbecue is particularly fun when you're cooking for a crowd. I like to go all out and serve some of the classic sides to go with the smoked meat: mac and cheese, braised collards or turnip greens, potato salad, coleslaw, beans, cornbread, and corn on the cob.

SMOKED PORK RIBS

During the spring and summer at our house, most large get-togethers involve firing up the smokehouse for some good old-fashioned barbecue. In our home, pork ribs are where it's at. There is something so satisfying about the process of making and eating them; we have been known to load up our smokehouse with upwards of 20 racks of ribs. The great thing about ribs is I can sleep in, go to the farmer's market, and come home with enough time to have smoked pork ribs for dinner. They are perfect for a grill table, aboveground pit, hot-smoke drum smoker, or smokehouse (as long as it is built for hot smoking).

Serves 2 people

- 2 tablespoons rub
  (see pages 88 to 90)
- 1 rack pork ribs, spare or
  baby back
- ⅓ cup barbecue sauce

1. An hour or so before smoking, apply the rub to your ribs (about 1 tablespoon per side). You want a nice even coat, with the meat still visible beneath the rub. Fill a spray bottle with water, cider vinegar, or whiskey.

2. Place the ribs, bone side down, in the smoker at a temperature between 225° and 250°F (110° and 120°C). Place a pan of water below or near the ribs to help keep moisture in the air.

3. Every hour or so, check the ribs. Spray the ribs with what's in your spray bottle to wash away any soot, and so that you can see the color that the ribs are turning. You'll know they are ready for barbecue sauce application when they have achieved a deep reddish-brown color throughout. They should be this color after about 3 hours.

4. Once the ribs have achieved the right color, lightly coat the first side with barbecue sauce. Let them smoke for 15 more minutes. Flip the ribs and coat the other side with barbecue sauce. Let smoke for another 15 minutes.

5. Wrap the ribs in foil and return to the smoker for about 1 hour. The ribs are ready when you can pick them up from the center and each side bends down limply. Too stiff and they aren't ready, but if they are too floppy and they just fall apart they are overdone (not the worst thing in the world). Different people like their ribs different textures, so experiment to see what level of chew you like. There is no wrong way.

6. Let rest, wrapped in foil, for 30 minutes and then serve.

SMOKED PORK SHOULDER

It doesn't get much better than smoked pork shoulder. It's great with a mustard-based sauce, a vinegar-based sauce, or a tomato-based sauce, on white bread, on sweet brioche, or just in a pile on your plate. Plus smoking a pork shoulder is a great way to spend a summer day in your backyard. Pork shoulders are perfect for a kettle grill (as long as it's a small chunk of shoulder), aboveground pit, hot-smoke drum smoker, or smokehouse (as long as it is built for hot smoking).

1. An hour or so before smoking, apply the rub to the pork shoulder. You want a nice even coat, with the meat still visible beneath the rub. Fill a spray bottle with water, cider vinegar, or whiskey.

2. Place the pork shoulder, fat side up, in the smoker at a temperature between 225° and 275°F (110° and 135°C). Place a pan of water below or near the shoulder to help keep moisture in the air. Smoke for 6 to 8 hours, occasionally checking the shoulder and spraying with your spray bottle to see the color of the meat. (If you want to apply a barbecue sauce to the shoulder while smoking — I don't usually do this, preferring to sauce it on my plate — it is ready for barbecue sauce application when the shoulder has achieved a deep reddish-brown color throughout, with a nice crusty bark.) You know the shoulder is done when you can easily pull out any bones or can easily separate the meat with your finger. You are looking for an internal temperature of 200°F (95°C).

3. Pull the shoulder out of the smoker and tent with aluminum foil. Let rest for 30 minutes. Pull the meat apart with your hands or chop up with a knife and serve with barbecue sauce.

Serves 10 people

- ⅓ cup rub (see pages 88 to 90)
- 1 5- to 7-pound pork shoulder (skin on or off, bone in or out)
  Barbecue sauce

SMOKED BRISKET

Smoking a brisket is a labor of love and a test of patience. The cook time for a brisket, assuming you eat dinner sometime between 5:30 and 8:30 PM, requires that you wake up early and get to work. This is something we only do once or twice a summer and then we go all out. If you have the smoker going all day, you might as well smoke some chicken, ribs, sausage, and pork shoulder too, right? These days often involve a lot of cold beer and a couple of sun-soaked naps. And once you have eaten the brisket, you'll fall straight into a food/beer/heat coma that lasts as long as the brisket took to smoke. Brisket is perfect for an aboveground pit, in-ground pit, hot-smoke drum smoker, or smokehouse (as long as it is built for hot smoking).

Serves 12 to 14 people

- 1 whole brisket, untrimmed (12 to 14 pounds)
- ½ cup beef barbecue rub (see page 90)

1. I like to leave most of the fat on a brisket, but if you prefer it trimmed, be sure to leave at least ¼ inch of fat on the fat cap side. If there is no fat on your brisket, it's not worth smoking.

2. Apply all of the rub about an hour before smoking. Fill a spray bottle with water, cider vinegar, or whiskey.

3. Place your brisket, fat side up, in a smoker that is at a temperature between 225° and 275°F (110° and 135°C). Place a pan of water below or near the brisket to help keep moisture in the air. Smoke for 4 to 6 hours, but after 3 hours, start to check for color by spritzing with your spray bottle (this also helps keep it moist). You're looking for a deep brown color. Once the brisket has a nice dark brown (nearly black) bark and has an internal temperature of about 165°F (74°C), take the brisket out and wrap in heavy-duty aluminum foil or butcher's paper.

4. Return the brisket to the smoker and continue cooking until they have an internal temperature of 200°F (95°C) and the meat is tender enough to pierce with your finger. This should take another 2 hours or so.

5. Keep the brisket wrapped and let it rest for 1 to 2 hours; longer is better. Trim away any unwanted fat, slice, and serve.

THE STALL

When you smoke large cuts like brisket, you'll encounter what's called "the stall": the period in which the cooking temperature on large cuts of meat plateaus, or stalls, for what feels like an agonizing and absurd amount of time. In the first part of the smoking period, the internal temperature of the meat continues to rise, as you would expect. Then, at around 160° to 170°F (70° to 77°C), it just stops rising. The stall has been the downfall of many brisket smokers; I fell victim to it myself the first time I tried smoking a brisket.

It happens because of something called "evaporative cooling." It is kind of like the process of sweating. Sweat cools down the human body by creating moisture that sits on the surface of your skin. The moisture is evaporated by the heat given off by your body. As the moisture on your skin transforms from a liquid to a gas, it absorbs a large amount of heat from your skin, which results in a cooling effect.

Inside your smoker, the piece of meat is essentially sweating, too: it's losing moisture through evaporation from the surface of the meat. The evaporative cooling effect will continue to affect the meat until all of the moisture has been completely evaporated from it — something that we don't want to happen to our food. No one wants a big dry piece of brisket! This is why we remove the meat from the smoker and wrap it for last stretch of smoking, sometimes referred to as "the Texas crutch," once the meat has reached its stall temperature. Wrapping the meat prevents evaporation and creates a cooking environment similar to a braise. The moisture stays trapped in the meat, while the collagen in the meat continues to break down. Some people worry that by wrapping the brisket they're losing out on a smoky flavor, but at this point in the smoking process, your meat is unlikely to get any smokier.

PIT-ROASTED WHOLE PIG, YUCATECAN STYLE (COCHINITA PIBIL)

One of the things that keeps bringing my wife and me back to the Yucatán is the incredible culinary tradition there. When I think of Yucatecan food, the first thing that comes to mind is cochinita pibil, *"little pig cooked in a pit." The brightness of the sour orange and lime juice, the slight bitterness of achiote, the earthy sweetness of the spices, and the intoxicating tea-like aroma of the charred banana leaves come together in the most amazing way. We only cook in a pit once or twice a year, and although it takes a lot of work and planning, we think it's well worth it, especially for a party.*

Serves 50 people

- 1 **6-inch stick cinnamon**
- ¾ **cup achiote seeds** (also called annatto)
- 3 **tablespoons black peppercorns**
- 3 **tablespoons allspice berries**
- 1½ **tablespoons cumin seeds**
- 60 **garlic cloves, skins on**
- ¼ **cup dried Mexican oregano**
- 1½ **cups fresh lime juice**
- ¾ **cup fresh orange juice**
- 1 **cup fine sea salt or kosher salt**
- 1 **small roaster pig** (40 to 60 pounds)
- 7 to 10 **banana leaves**

1. In a dry cast-iron pan, lightly toast the cinnamon, achiote seeds, peppercorns, allspice berries, and cumin seeds over medium heat for about 5 minutes, or until the spices begin to release their aromas and start to look a little toasted. Let cool, then grind the spices in a spice grinder.

2. In the same pan, roast the garlic cloves over medium heat until softened and lightly blackened in spots, about 6 minutes. Set aside and let cool. Once cooled, remove the garlic from the skins.

3. Combine the ground spices, garlic, oregano, and lime and orange juices in a blender and purée until smooth. This is your marinade. Rub the marinade and the salt all over the pig and let sit overnight in your fridge.

4. Prepare your pit by creating a bed of hot coals 1 to 2 feet thick.

5. Wrap the pig in banana leaves. I like to secure the banana leaves around the pig using butcher's twine or wire. Once your pit is ready, gently place the banana leaf–wrapped pig in the pit and cover the pit.

6. Wait 8 to 12 hours, then check your pig: the skin should be stiff and browned, achiote paste should be a deep reddish-brown color, and the meat should pull away from the bone. Serve with tortillas, pickled red onions, and habanero salsa.

BEEF RIBS

Smoking beef ribs is very similar to smoking beef brisket. These are especially fun to do if you can get your butcher to cut them long for you — like 8 to 12 inches long. You can smoke the ribs as individual ribs, or you can have your butcher leave them as one large rack that you carve when done. These are sometimes called dinosaur ribs, like what Fred Flintstone eats at the drive-in. And, as the nickname implies, eating these gives one a primal thrill. It is very satisfying holding up a large rib and gnawing away at, and the flavor the meat takes on, from being on the bone, is fantastic. Beef ribs are perfect for the aboveground pit, hot-smoke drum smoker, or smokehouse (as long as it is built for hot smoking).

Serves 3

¼ cup beef barbecue rub
(see page 90)

1 three-bone rack of beef plate short ribs (around 5 pounds)

1. Apply all of the rub to the ribs about an hour before smoking. Fill a spray bottle with water, cider vinegar, or whiskey.

2. Place your ribs, fat side up, in a smoker that is at a temperature between 225° and 275°F (110° and 135°C). Place a pan of water below or near the ribs to help keep moisture in the air. Smoke for 4 to 6 hours, but after about 3 hours, start to check for color by spritzing with your spray bottle (this also helps keep it moist). You're looking for a deep brown. Once the ribs have a nice dark brown (nearly black) bark and an internal temperature of about 165°F (74°C), take the ribs out of the smoker and wrap in heavy-duty aluminum foil or butcher's paper.

3. Return the ribs to the smoker and continue cooking until they have an internal temperature of 200°F (95°C) and the meat is tender enough to pierce with your finger. This should take another 2 hours or so.

4. Keep the ribs wrapped and let them rest for 1 hour before serving.

SMOKEHOUSE BEANS

Beans are a perfect partner for barbecue. The night before I plan to fire up the smokehouse, I set some black beans or pinto beans out to soak. Then, before I get the fire going in Frazier, I throw the beans in my big cast-iron kettle with some water, garlic, and an onion and bring them to a boil. Once the fire in my smokehouse is going, the beans go in. Although they aren't overwhelmingly smoky, they do pick up some of the flavor from being in the smoker.

Serves 12

- 4 cups dried beans (black or pinto)
- 1 medium yellow onion (skin on), cut in half
- 1 head garlic (skin on)
- 1 bay leaf
- 1 cup barbecue sauce (optional)

1. Soak the beans in cold water overnight. The water level should be about 4 inches above the beans.

2. Drain the soaked beans and put them in a heavy pot or Dutch oven. I like to use my cast-iron kettle. Pour in enough cold water to just cover the beans. Add the onion, garlic, and bay leaf and bring to a boil on your kitchen stove.

3. Move the pot of beans to the smoker and continue to cook. The beans should be gently simmering. Keep an eye on the pot. If the beans begin to dry out while cooking, add a cup of hot water.

4. Cook until the beans are just tender, usually about 3 hours. Remove the onion, garlic, and bay leaf. Stir in barbecue sauce, if using, and serve.

BACON

I've talked to many people who say, "Oh, I'm a vegetarian. Well, except for bacon . . ." or "I try to keep kosher, but bacon doesn't count." I mean, who doesn't love bacon? It is a totally unrivaled food item. Bacon is a key ingredient in much of my cooking: for breakfast, as a base for a sauce, and in soups, stir-fries, rice and beans, and cooked greens. And the only thing more satisfying than opening up your fridge and seeing a good supply of bacon is opening up your fridge and seeing bacon you cured and smoked yourself.

Bacon is also one of those foods that invites lots of experimentation and play. The belly takes on flavors exceptionally well. While classic bacon is fantastic, it's really fun to try other flavor profiles. I tend to smoke a few bellies at a time in a variety of styles, like Sichuan bacon, miso-honey bacon, chorizo bacon, Thai-style bacon, Calabrian bacon, and so many more. Once they're done, I cut them up into 4- to 8-ounce pieces, wrap them, label them, and put them in the freezer until needed. Bacon is best made in a hot-smoke drum smoker or smokehouse.

CLASSIC BACON

For this classic bacon recipe, I use maple syrup or maple sugar, but any sweetener works well.

1. To make the cure, combine the sea salt, curing salt, and brown sugar and mix thoroughly. Rub the cure over the entire surface of the belly. Place the belly, with any excess cure mixture, in a nonreactive container just big enough to fit the belly. The belly will release liquid during the curing process, creating a brine. It's important that the meat keeps in contact with the brine throughout the curing process.

2. Refrigerate, flipping the belly every other day, for 7 to 10 days. The meat should be firm to the touch, like a well-done steak or pork chop.

3. Remove the belly from the cure and rinse it thoroughly under cold water. Rub it dry with a clean cloth. Place the meat on a rack set on a sheet pan and let rest in your fridge, uncovered, for at least 12 hours but no longer than 24 hours.

4. Place the belly, skin side up, in the smoker or, if possible, hang from a bacon hook at a temperature between 150° and 200°F (65° and 95°C). Smoke until the bacon reaches an internal temperature of 150°F (65°C), about 3 hours.

5. Remove the belly from the smoker and peel off the skin; start with a knife to release the skin on one side and then it should easily peel off by hand from there. If you're having trouble, use a knife to peel off all of the skin, but be sure to leave as much fat as possible on the bacon.

6. Let the bacon cool to room temperature. Once cooled, wrap in butcher's paper or plastic wrap and refrigerate overnight. Then it is ready to be sliced and cooked or frozen as needed.

Makes 10 pounds

⅓ cup/135 grams fine sea salt or kosher salt (3% of weight of meat)

Cure #1 or Veg Stable 504 (use supplier's recommended quantity for 10 pounds of meat)

⅓ cup/68 grams brown sugar (firmly packed), maple syrup, granulated sugar, or honey (1.5% of weight of meat)

1 10-pound/4.5-kilogram fresh pork belly, skin on

SICHUAN BACON

I love the interplay of spicy Sichuan peppercorns and chiles with the warm and sweet spices used in most Sichuan cuisine. (I've also become addicted to the tingly, numbing feeling that Sichuan peppers give your mouth.) These bold, aromatic flavors lend themselves perfectly to bacon. The mouth-numbing effect of the Sichuan pepper gets a little lost during the curing process, which is why I like to apply a rub of ground Sichuan pepper before smoking this bacon. I developed this recipe based on Fuchsia Dunlop's recipe for Sichuan bacon in her book Land of Plenty.

1. To make the cure, combine the sea salt, curing salt, brown sugar, ¼ cup of the Sichuan pepper, wine, cloves, and star anise, mixing thoroughly. Rub the cure over the entire surface of the belly. Place the belly, with any excess cure, in a nonreactive container just big enough to fit the belly. The belly will release liquid during the curing process, creating a brine. It's important that the meat keeps in contact with the brine throughout the curing process.

2. Refrigerate, flipping the belly every other day, for 7 to 10 days, until the meat is firm to the touch.

3. Remove the belly from the cure and rinse it thoroughly under cold water. Pat it dry with a clean cloth. Place the meat on a rack on a sheet pan and let rest in your fridge, uncovered, for at least 12 hours but no more than 24 hours.

4. Rub the remaining ¼ cup of ground Sichuan pepper into the meat of the belly. Place the belly, skin side up, in the smoker or, if possible, hang from a bacon hook at a temperature between 150° and 200°F (65° and 95°C). Smoke until the bacon reaches an internal temperature of 150°F (65°C), about 3 hours.

5. Remove the belly from the smoker and peel off the skin; start with a knife to release the skin on one side and then it should easily peel off by hand from there. If you're having trouble, use a knife to peel off all of the skin, but be sure to leave as much fat as possible on the bacon.

6. Let cool to room temperature. Once cooled, wrap in butcher's paper or plastic wrap and refrigerate overnight. Then it is ready to be sliced and cooked or frozen as needed.

Makes 10 pounds

- ⅓ cup/135 grams fine sea salt or kosher salt (3% of weight of meat)
- Cure #1 or Veg Stable 504 (use supplier's recommended quantity for 10 pounds of meat)
- ¼ cup/45 grams dark brown sugar (packed firmly) or honey (1% of weight of meat)
- ½ cup/45 grams ground Sichuan pepper (1% of weight of meat)
- ¼ cup/45 grams Shaoxing rice wine (1% of weight of meat)
- 2 teaspoons/5 grams ground cloves (0.1% of weight of meat)
- 4 teaspoons/5 grams ground star anise (0.1% of weight of meat)
- 1 10-pound/4.5-kilogram fresh pork belly, skin on

LAMB, MUTTON, GOAT, OR VENISON BACON

Like "shamb" (see page 101), this recipe came out of the experimenting my colleagues and I did at the Meat Market with Kinderhook mutton. When developing this recipe, we thought about the ingredients we often use when cooking with lamb. This bacon is more of a savory bacon than a sweet one, and it lends itself more to being used as a flavoring ingredient than to just eating it as is. It's also a fun alternative for people who don't eat pork. This is a great addition to any stew or chili.

Makes 4½ pounds

- 3 tablespoons/60 grams fine sea salt or kosher salt (3% of weight of meat)
  Cure #1 or Veg Stable 504 (use supplier's recommended quantity for 4½ pounds of meat)
- 2 tablespoons/30 grams dark brown sugar (packed firmly), maple syrup, or honey (1.5% of weight of meat)
- 2 teaspoons/4 grams ground black pepper (0.2% of weight of meat)
- 2 tablespoons/2 grams fresh rosemary leaves (0.1% of weight of meat)
- 1 teaspoon/2 grams minced garlic (0.1% of weight of meat)
- 1 4½-pound/2-kilogram fresh lamb, mutton, goat, or venison belly

1. To make the cure, combine the sea salt, curing salt, brown sugar, black pepper, rosemary, and garlic, mixing thoroughly. Rub the cure over the entire surface of the belly. Place the belly, with any excess cure, in a nonreactive container just big enough to fit the belly. The belly will release liquid during the curing process, creating a brine. It's important that the meat keeps in contact with the brine throughout the curing process.

2. Refrigerate, flipping the belly every other day, for 2 to 3 days, until the meat is firm to the touch.

3. Remove the belly from the cure and rinse it thoroughly under cold water. Pat it dry with a clean cloth. Place the meat on a rack on a sheet pan and let rest, uncovered, in your fridge for at least 12 hours but no more than 24 hours.

4. Roll the belly, lengthwise, as tightly as you can and tie it, so that it is a more or less an even thickness throughout. Place the rolled and tied belly in the smoker at a temperature between 150° and 200°F (65° and 95°C). Smoke until the bacon has reached an internal temperature of 150°F (65°C), about 3 hours.

5. Remove the belly from the smoker and let cool to room temperature. Once cooled, wrap in butcher's paper or plastic wrap and refrigerate overnight. Then it is ready to be sliced and cooked or frozen as needed.

HOT-SMOKED SAUSAGES

Whenever I am at a loss for what to make for dinner, I almost always fall back on sausage. With a side of greens and some potatoes, polenta, or rice, you have a simple and delicious meal. But on those nights when I can't even be bothered to spend *that* much time cooking, I reach in my fridge for a smoked sausage, throw it on the grill or in the oven to warm it up, and serve it as is. I also use smoked sausages as a flavoring ingredient, especially for paella, gumbo, a soup, or a stir-fry. One of our easy, go-to weeknight recipes is a Spanish tortilla or frittata with smoked sausage, onions, and potatoes.

As with bacon, I make 10 pounds or more of the sausage at a time, then pack and freeze it for later use. Often, I try to coordinate smoking sausage with other meats, like ribs or a pork shoulder, and do it all in my smokehouse in one day. But it is also just as easy to fire up my hot-smoke drum smoker and make a small batch of sausage in an afternoon.

KIELBASA

Here in western Massachusetts we have a large Polish-American population, and with that comes kielbasa — a garlicky smoked sausage that is perfect with bread, mustard, and sauerkraut. When I was growing up, this was a standard food in our house, especially when my dad was cooking. In eastern Europe you'll find dozens of variations of kielbasa: different spice mixtures, combinations of meats, diameters, kinds of smokes. This recipe is based on the classic kielbasas I grew up eating — heavy on the garlic, with a hint of sweetness.

Makes 10 1-pound links

- 10 pounds/4.5 kilograms pork trim (about 70% lean and 30% fat)
- 3½ tablespoons/68 grams fine sea salt or kosher salt (1.5% of weight of meat)
- Cure #1 or Veg Stable 504 (use supplier's recommended quantity for 10 pounds of meat)
- 1 tablespoon/10 grams minced garlic (0.2% of weight of meat)
- 2½ teaspoons/7.5 grams ground black pepper (0.17% of weight of meat)
- 1 teaspoon/3 grams ground coriander (0.07% of weight of meat)
- 1 teaspoon/3 grams dried marjoram (0.07% of weight)
- 1 teaspoon/3 grams sweet paprika (0.07% of weight of meat)
- 15 feet 32- to 35-millimeter hog casings, soaked in tepid water for at least 30 minutes

1. Grind the meat through a well-chilled ¼-inch (6-millimeter) grinder plate. Mix in the sea salt, curing salt, garlic, black pepper, coriander, marjoram, and paprika thoroughly, either by hand or using an electric stand mixer with the paddle attachment, so that the meat becomes sticky and the spices are evenly distributed. Chill the batter until it's below 40°F (4.5°C), but not frozen.

2. Stuff the batter into the prepared casings and form into 6- to 12-inch links, leaving the links attached.

3. Place the links on a drying rack on a sheet pan in the refrigerator and let dry overnight.

4. Hang the sausages over a smoke stick and smoke between 170° and 200°F (77° and 95°C). Smoke until the sausages reach an internal temperature of 150°F (65°C), about 1 hour.

5. Let rest for 30 minutes and serve, or store in refrigerator for up to 7 days, or freeze.

MAKING SAUSAGE

Making sausage is a craft in and of itself. It can feel a little awkward at first, but it's really fun and satisfying once you get the hang of it. One key to the process is having a good meat grinder and stuffer. You can buy meat grinding and stuffing attachments for your electric stand mixer, but if you think you'll spend a fair amount of time making sausage, I highly recommending buying an actual meat grinder. I also have a separate sausage stuffer, but most meat grinders come with stuffing attachments that work perfectly well.

Grinding and Mixing

1. Choose your meat. Shoulder is the most commonly used cut. The fat content of the sausage should be at least 20 percent; it's best at 30 percent, which happens to be the natural amount found in a shoulder.

2. Cut, weigh, and freeze. Cube the meat according to your grinder feed-tube size. Weigh your meat. Chill the meat, along with the grinding plate (die size can vary depending on your setup and preference; I prefer ³⁄₁₆ inch), blade, auger, and grinder throat, in a freezer for about 30 minutes.

3. Grind. Run the meat through the grinder.

4. Weigh out and mix in salt and spices. Weigh out and mix together the sea salt, curing salt, spices, and herbs. Then mix the cure into the ground meat thoroughly with your hands or an electric stand mixer fitted with a paddle at medium speed, until the spices and herbs are evenly incorporated and the mixture is sticky — it is sticky enough when it sticks to your hands.

5. Refrigerate. Store the batter in your refrigerator until you are ready to case the sausage.

Stuffing

6. Prepare the casing. I like to use natural hog casings in the 32- to 35-millimeter size range for most fresh and smoked sausages and in the 42- to 44-millimeter size for dry-cured sausages. To prepare the casings, untangle them and rinse thoroughly. Soak the casings in tepid (100°F/38°C) water for at least 30 minutes before using.

7. Set up the stuffer. Wet the plunger, the walls of the chamber, and stuffing tube to make your stuffing experience smoother. Load the batter into the stuffer and pack it well, avoiding air pockets in the stuffer chamber.

8. Load the casing. Slide the casing onto the stuffing tube.

9. Stuff slowly. Control the density of sausage by providing resistance to the casing on the stuffing tube. Do not overstuff; the casing should not be taut or else you will not be able to link it.

Making Links

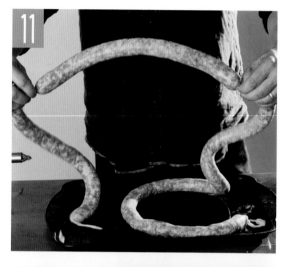

10. Measure and pinch. Measure the length you want for the sausage link and pinch the sausage gently at the desired length.

11. Link the sausage. Make the link by twisting in a forward direction for about five rotations. Then measure and pinch the end of the next link. When you form this second link, twist the sausage backward. Repeat this process, alternating forward and backward, until all of the sausage is linked.

12. Pierce air pockets. Watch for air pockets and prick any significant pockets with a sausage pricker.

Drying and Smoking

13. Dry the sausages. Place the sausages on a rack on a sheet pan, uncovered, in the refrigerator overnight to allow the surfaces to dry out and develop a pellicle.

14. Smoke the sausages. Hang the sausages from smoke sticks (see below) in your smoker. Smoke between 170° and 200°F (77° and 95°C). Smoke until the sausage has reached an internal temperature of 150°F (66°C), about 1 hour.

15. Let rest. Let the sausages rest for 30 minutes. Now they are ready to eat or to be cooked. You can store them in the fridge for up to 7 days or freeze them.

HANG YOUR SAUSAGES TO SMOKE

To properly smoke your sausages, you'll want to buy or make some smoke sticks. These are generally made from rebar or angle iron fit to the size of your smoker. They are literally just sticks for the sausages, still linked together, to hang from in the smoker. Hanging them this way ensures that all of the sausages get evenly smoked and don't pick up marks or discoloration from lying on a grill grate. If you don't hang your sausages from a smoke stick, make sure that the sausages are not in contact with one another; any place where they are touching will be a spot where smoke is not able to penetrate.

LINGUIÇA

One of the great things Portuguese immigrants brought to this country is linguiça — a sausage that features the classic, mouthwatering Iberian combination of garlic, paprika, and pork. Add a kiss of smoke to it, and you're in heaven. Linguiça is superb with eggs or in a kale and potato soup. It is also great in a Portuguese roll with some aioli and roasted or pickled peppers.

1. Grind the meat through a well-chilled ¼-inch (6-millimeter) grinder plate. Mix in the sea salt, curing salt, black pepper, paprika, garlic, sugar, coriander, cumin, and red pepper flakes thoroughly, either by hand or using an electric stand mixer with the paddle attachment at medium speed, so that the meat becomes sticky and the spices are evenly distributed. Chill the batter, until it's below 40°F (4.5°C), but not frozen.

2. Stuff the batter into the prepared casings and form into 6-inch links, leaving the links attached.

3. Place the links on a drying rack on a sheet pan in the refrigerator and let dry overnight.

4. Hang the sausages over a smoke stick and smoke between 170° and 200°F (77° and 95°C). Smoke until the sausages reach an internal temperature of 150°F (65°C), about 1 hour.

5. Let rest for 30 minutes and serve, or store in refrigerator for up to 7 days, or freeze.

Makes 10 1-pound links

- 10 pounds/4.5 kilograms pork trim (about 70% lean and 30% fat)
- 3½ tablespoons/68 grams fine sea salt or kosher salt (1.5% of weight of meat)
- Cure #1 or Veg Stable 504 (use supplier's recommended quantity for 10 pounds of meat)
- ¼ cup/30 grams ground black pepper (0.6% of weight of meat)
- 3 tablespoons/30 grams sweet paprika (0.6% of weight of meat)
- 1½ tablespoons/15 grams minced garlic (0.3% of weight of meat)
- 1 tablespoon/15 grams sugar (0.3% of weight of meat)
- 2 teaspoons/5 grams ground coriander (0.1% of weight of meat)
- 2 teaspoons/5 grams ground cumin (0.1% of weight of meat)
- 2 teaspoons/5 grams red pepper flakes (0.1% of weight of meat)
- 15 feet 32- to 35-millimeter hog casings, soaked in tepid water for at least 30 minutes

ANDOUILLE

Another classic hot-smoked sausage is American in its roots: the Cajun andouille sausage. Like American barbecue, this sausage is the result of various cultures (Spanish, French, Native American) melting together in the American South, in this case in Louisiana. I'm not sure where my family's love of Cajun food comes from, but at large family celebrations or special occasions it's not uncommon for my parents or my brother Sam to make a gumbo or jambalaya. Neither dish would be complete without this sausage.

1. Grind the meat through a well-chilled ¼-inch (6-millimeter) grinder plate. Mix in the sea salt, curing salt, onion powder, black pepper, cayenne, garlic, green bell pepper, red pepper flakes, bay leaves, marjoram, thyme, mace, allspice, and cloves and mix thoroughly, either by hand or using an electric stand mixer with the paddle attachment on medium speed, so that the meat becomes sticky and the spices are evenly distributed. Chill the batter until it's below 40°F (4.5°C), but not frozen.

2. Stuff the batter into the prepared casings and form into 6- to 12-inch links, leaving the links attached.

3. Place the links in your fridge on a drying rack on a sheet pan and let dry overnight.

4. Hang the sausages over a smoke stick and smoke between 170° and 200°F (77° and 95°C). Smoke until the sausages reach an internal temperature of 150°F (65°C).

5. Let rest for 30 minutes and serve, or store in refrigerator for up to 7 days, or freeze.

Makes 10 1-pound links

- 10 pounds/4.5 kilograms pork trim (about 70% lean and 30% fat)
- 3½ tablespoons/68 grams fine sea salt or kosher salt (1.5% of weight of meat)
- Cure #1 or Veg Stable 504 (use supplier's recommended quantity for 10 pounds of meat)
- 2 tablespoons/15 grams onion powder (0.3% of weight of meat)
- 1 tablespoon/10 grams ground black pepper (0.2% of weight of meat)
- 1 tablespoon/10 grams cayenne pepper (0.2% of weight of meat)
- 1 tablespoon/10 grams minced garlic (0.2% of weight of meat)
- 1 tablespoon/10 grams finely chopped green bell pepper (0.2% of weight of meat)
- 1 tablespoon/5 grams red pepper flakes (0.1% of weight of meat)
- 2 tablespoons/5 grams ground bay leaves (0.1% of weight of meat)
- 2 tablespoons/5 grams dried marjoram (0.1% of weight of meat)
- 2 tablespoons/5 grams dried thyme (0.1% of weight of meat)
- 2 teaspoons/5 grams ground allspice (0.1% of weight of meat)
- 2 teaspoons/5 grams ground cloves (0.1% of weight of meat)
- 2 teaspoons/5 grams ground mace (0.1% of weight of meat)
- 15 feet 32- to 35-millimeter hog casings, soaked in tepid water for at least 30 minutes

COLD-SMOKING RECIPES

Cold smoking is too often overshadowed by its more popular sibling, hot smoking, but it's a fantastic technique that results in some of the world's greatest food delicacies. Traditionally cold smoking is applied to cured meats like hams and dry-cured sausages and delicate fish like salmon. While hot smoking cooks the meat, cold smoking flavors and preserves the meat without cooking it. Because cold smoking is about adding a smoky flavor and preserving the meat, it often takes place over a longer period of time than hot smoking, lasting for days or even weeks in some cases.

COLD-SMOKING BASICS

Before putting meat in a cold smoker, it needs to be cured. This is as much a matter of food safety as it is a matter of flavor. The application of salt and nitrites allows the meat to be safely held despite being at temperatures in which harmful bacteria normally thrive. The addition of salt also has many positive effects on the flavor and texture of the meat.

BASIC CURE FOR COLD-SMOKED MEAT

This is a basic cure recipe on which you can build with other spices and herbs.

1. Mix together the sea salt, sugar, and curing salt. Completely coat the meat in this mixture. Place the meat in a nonreactive container, pour in any excess cure, cover, and cure in the refrigerator, allowing 1 day for every 2 pounds (1 kilogram) of meat.

2. Rinse under cold water and dry off with a clean dish towel, rubbing the surface of the meat vigorously. Place on a rack on a sheet pan and let it rest, uncovered, in your refrigerator until surface is dry and slightly tacky, around 12 hours.

Fine sea salt or kosher salt (2% of weight of meat)

Sugar (0.66% of weight of meat)

Cure #1 or Veg Stable 504 (use supplier's recommended quantity)

SMOKED SALMON

This cure is a very simple one, but feel free to build on it with ½ teaspoon of spices or herbs like mace, allspice, bay leaves, ground chiles, thyme, and so on. Cold-smoked cured fish doesn't typically require curing salt, but if you prefer to use it here, you certainly may (follow the manufacturer's specifications). This recipe also works well with trout, cod, pollock, and haddock.

Serves 4 to 6 people

- ½ cup/150 grams fine sea salt or kosher salt
- ¼ cup/75 grams dark brown sugar, firmly packed
- ¼ cup/75 grams granulated white sugar
- 1 teaspoon ground white pepper
- 1 1½-pound/68-kilogram salmon fillet, skin on, pin bones removed
- 1½ tablespoons dark rum

1. Mix together the salt, brown sugar, white sugar, and white pepper.

2. In a nonreactive pan, just big enough to fit the salmon fillet, spread half of the cure in an even layer in the same dimensions as the fillet. Place the salmon, skin side down, in the cure. Sprinkle the rum over the fillet, then coat the fillet with the rest of the cure. The cure should be thicker over the thickest part of the fillet, and thinner on the thin ends of the fillet.

3. Cover the salmon with plastic wrap and set another pan on the fillet. Place some heavy objects on the pan (about 10 pounds total). Refrigerate for 36 hours, or until the thickest part of the fillet feels firm to the touch.

4. Remove the salmon from the cure and rinse under cool water. Pat dry. Place the salmon on a rack set on a sheet pan, skin side down, and refrigerate, uncovered, for at least a few hours, and up to 1 day.

5. Cold smoke the salmon, skin side down, for about 6 hours, or to taste.

6. Store in the refrigerator for up to a week. To serve, slice thinly at an angle, carving it off the skin.

FOR THE LOVE OF LOX

One of the most well-known traditions of my eastern European Jewish heritage is lox, or smoked salmon. Special occasions are marked by an iridescent orange side of smoked salmon, a basket of warm bagels, wedges of lemons, thinly sliced red onions, a bowl of briny capers, and a big tub of cream cheese. Given our ancestral connection to this cold-smoked food item, it seemed fitting that this was the very first thing we smoked in our smokehouse — and it didn't disappoint. If only finances and time allowed, I would smoke a side of salmon every week for my family to eat on Sunday mornings. Maybe someday.

COLD-SMOKED BACON

Cold-smoked bacon is more shelf stable than hot-smoked bacon, and some people prefer the cold-smoked bacon flavor to that of the traditional hot smoked — it can have a richer and more nuanced flavor because it's been dry cured rather than cooked. Cold smoking also allows you to build a smokier flavor profile, as you can leave something in the cold smoker for as long as you want because there is no concern about it overcooking or drying out. The longer it is exposed to smoke, the deeper the smoke flavor will be. Another nice benefit to cold-smoked bacon is that you don't have to freeze it. The bacon should last a long time just in the fridge, as long as it is well wrapped.

ENGLISH BACON

This basic cold-smoked recipe is inspired by traditional English bacon, and although this cure is usually applied to back bacon (the loin with some of the belly on it), it works great on just a belly.

Makes 10 pounds

⅓ cup/135 grams fine sea salt or kosher salt (3% of weight of meat)

Cure #1 or Veg Stable 504 (use supplier's recommended quantity for 10 pounds of meat)

¼ cup/68 grams blackstrap molasses (1.5% of weight of meat)

2 tablespoons/20 grams ground black pepper (0.4% of weight of meat)

1 teaspoon/2 grams juniper berries, bruised (0.04% of weight of meat)

5 bay leaves/1 gram (0.02% of weight of meat)

1 10-pound/4.5-kilogram fresh pork belly, skin on

1. To make the cure, combine the sea salt, curing salt, molasses, pepper, juniper berries, and bay leaves, mixing thoroughly.

2. Rub the cure over the entire surface of the belly. Place the belly with any excess cure, in a nonreactive container just big enough to fit it. The belly will release liquid during the curing process, creating a brine. It's important that the meat keeps contact with the brine throughout the curing process.

3. Refrigerate, flipping the belly every other day, for 7 to 10 days, until the meat is firm to the touch.

4. Remove the belly from the cure and rinse it thoroughly under cold water. Dry it vigorously with a clean cloth. Place it on a rack on a sheet pan and let rest, uncovered, in the refrigerator for at least 12 hours and up to 24 hours.

5. Place the belly, skin side up, in the cold smoker or, if possible, hang from a bacon hook. Cold smoke for about 12 hours.

6. Remove the belly from the smoker and hang in a cool (32° to 55°F/0° to 13°C), dark environment for a minimum of 5 days, and up to 3 months, to allow it to further dry.

7. Remove the skin with a sharp knife. Slice and cook as you would hot-smoked bacon. To store, wrap it in plastic wrap or vacuum-pack it and keep it in your fridge for up to 3 months.

MISO-HONEY BACON

The combination of miso and honey is the perfect balance of funk, sweet, and salt. I use them on roasted root vegetables and squash and as a simple glaze for salmon and pork. I have also always loved garlic and honey together — one of my favorite bacons we make at Jacuterie (the salumerie where I work) is garlic honey, and I figured that those flavors all together would make a great bacon. I will humbly admit to being right. I like this bacon in BLTs, as lardons for salad, in a stir-fry, or in ramen.

Makes 10 pounds

- ¼ cup/90 grams fine sea salt or kosher salt (2% of weight of meat)
- Cure #1 or Veg Stable 504 (use supplier's recommended quantity for 10 pounds of meat)
- ¼ cup/90 grams honey (2% of weight of meat)
- ¼ cup/90 grams sweet white miso (2% of weight of meat)
- 6 tablespoons/90 grams minced garlic (2% of weight of meat)
- 1 10-pound/4.5-kilogram fresh pork belly, skin on

1. To make the cure, combine the sea salt, curing salt, honey, miso, and garlic, mixing thoroughly.

2. Rub the cure mixture over the entire surface of the belly. Place the belly with any excess cure in a nonreactive container just big enough to fit the belly. The belly will release liquid during the curing process, creating a brine. It's important that the meat keeps contact with the brine throughout the curing process.

3. Refrigerate, flipping the belly every other day, for 7 to 10 days, until the meat is firm to the touch.

4. Remove the belly from the cure and rinse it thoroughly under cold water. Dry it vigorously with a clean cloth. Place it on a rack on a sheet pan and let rest, uncovered, in the refrigerator for at least 12 hours and up to 24 hours.

5. Place the belly, skin side up, or if possible hanging from a bacon hook, in your cold smoker and smoke for about 12 hours.

6. Remove the belly from the smoker and hang in a cool (32° to 55°F/0° to 13°C), dark environment for a minimum of 5 days, and up to 3 months, to let further dry.

7. Remove the skin with a sharp knife. Slice and cook as you would hot-smoked bacon. To store, wrap it in plastic wrap or vacuum-pack it and keep it in your fridge for up to 3 months.

THAI RED CURRY BACON

In my never-ending quest to see how Southeast Asian flavor combinations can be blended with traditional Western cured meat products, I created this recipe. We made it as a limited-edition bacon at Jacuterie but didn't put it into regular production because it involves some ingredients that are tricky to source, and it's a little "out there." It's great in stir-fries, fried rice, soups, or a bacon–peanut butter–kimchi sandwich.

1. To make the cure, combine the sea salt, curing salt, sugar, chile peppers, garlic, coriander, cumin, galangal, white pepper, ginger, and lemongrass, mixing thoroughly.

2. Rub the cure mixture over the entire surface of the belly. Place the belly with any excess cure in a nonreactive container just big enough to fit the belly. The belly will release liquid during the curing process, creating a brine. It's important that the meat keeps contact with the brine throughout the curing process.

3. Refrigerate, flipping the belly every other day, for 7 to 10 days, until the meat is firm to the touch.

4. Remove the belly from the cure and rinse it thoroughly under cold water. Dry it vigorously with a clean cloth. Place it on a rack on a sheet pan and let rest, uncovered, in the refrigerator for at least 12 hours and up to 24 hours.

5. Place the belly, skin side up, in the cold smoker or, if possible, hang from a bacon hook. Smoke for about 12 hours.

6. Remove the belly from the smoker and hang in a cool (32° to 55°F/0° to 13°C), dark environment for a minimum of 5 days, and up to 3 months, to let further dry.

7. Remove the skin with a sharp knife. Slice and cook as you would hot-smoked bacon. To store, wrap it in plastic wrap, or vacuum pack it and keep it in your fridge for up to 3 months.

Makes 10 pounds

- ⅓ cup/135 grams fine sea salt or kosher salt (3% of weight of meat)
- Cure #1 or Veg Stable 504 (use supplier's recommended quantity for 10 pounds of meat)
- ¼ cup/68 grams granulated sugar, honey, or palm sugar (1.5% of weight of meat)
- 6 tablespoons/90 grams dried Thai chile peppers (bird chiles) (2% of weight of meat)
- 4½ tablespoons/45 grams minced garlic (1% of weight of meat)
- 3 tablespoons/23 grams ground coriander (0.5% of weight of meat)
- 3 tablespoons/23 grams ground cumin (0.5% of weight of meat)
- 3 tablespoons/23 grams ground dried galangal (0.5% of weight of meat; substitute ground ginger if you can't find galangal)
- 3 tablespoons/23 grams ground white pepper (0.5% of weight of meat)
- 1½ tablespoons/23 grams ground ginger (0.5% of weight of meat)
- 1½ tablespoons/23 grams dried lemongrass (0.5% of weight of meat)
- 1 10-pound/4.5-kilogram pork belly, skin on

COLD-SMOKED SAUSAGES

Cold smoking a sausage, as with cold smoking anything, comes with greater food safety risks. Making a cold-smoked sausage requires knowledge and a little experience with the process of making dry-cured sausages. It is important to have the space with the proper environmental conditions and equipment to ferment the sausage. But that isn't meant to scare you. While there is a learning curve, it is well worth working through it; just be mindful of the risks involved and follow the guidelines.

DRY-CURED SAUSAGES

Fermenting sausages to be dry-cured is a crucial step in making sure they're safe to eat. The fermentation lowers the pH in the sausage to below 5.3 — a level that is too acidic for many of the most dangerous bacteria like *E. coli* and listeria. The fermentation also adds a nice flavor to the sausage.

In order to properly ferment sausages, you need a clean space in which you can control both the temperature and humidity levels. My fermentation chamber is a large box made of a frame of 2×4s covered in 8-mil plastic with a heater and a humidifier in the bottom. I use my smoke sticks to hang the sausages in it, set the heater and humidifier to the right settings, and seal the box up for 24 hours.

To ensure that proper fermentation happens, you'll need to add a starter culture to the sausage mix. Depending on what kind of starter culture you use (I recommend B-LC-007), you'll need to ferment your sausage for various amounts of times at various temperatures. You want to bring the temperature of the fermentation chamber up to around 70°F (21°C) for 24 to 48 hours, at a humidity level of 80 to 90 percent, so the sausages don't dry.

If you don't have a pH meter, the easiest way to tell that the sausages are properly fermented is to check the color and texture of the meat; it should be bright pink and feel firm and bound together. In fact, it should feel like a cooked sausage, meaning it doesn't squish around the way the batter did when you first stuffed the sausage. I recommend investing in a pH meter if you're interested in producing dry-cured sausages regularly.

Once the sausage is fermented, you'll need to hang it to dry cure. This should also happen in a clean, pest-proof space in which the temperature and humidity can be controlled. The ideal dry-cure hanging conditions are a temperature of 55°F (12°C), 75 percent humidity, and a good airflow. I have created dedicated spaces in my basement for these processes — I'm lucky to have a basement that stays near 55°F (12°C) year-round. I have walled off one end of my basement and installed a fan and a dehumidifier/humidifier set at 75 percent humidity. This is my dry-curing cave and meat lab.

LANDJAEGER

This German venison and pork sausage is a classic cold-smoked, dry-cured sausage. The word jaeger *means "hunter" in German. No one knows for sure whether it's called a hunter's sausage because it utilizes wild meats (like wild boar or venison) or because this preserved sausage was traditionally brought on hunting trips since it lasts so long. Eat it with bread, cheese, mustard, pickles, and some good beer.*

Makes approximately 20 5-ounce dry-cured sausages

- 7 pounds/3 kilograms lean venison or beef, cubed and chilled
- 4 pounds, 6.5 ounces/ 2 kilograms fatty pork shoulder, cubed and chilled
- ¼ cup/100 grams fine sea salt or kosher salt (2% of weight of meat)
- Cure #2 or Veg Stable 504 (use supplier's recommended quantity for 11 pounds of meat)
- Starter culture (I use B-LC-007; use supplier's recommended quantity for 11 pounds of meat)
- 2½ tablespoons/25 grams ground black pepper (0.5% of weight of meat)
- 2 tablespoons/30 grams sugar (0.6% of weight of meat)
- 1½ tablespoons/15 grams minced garlic (0.3% of weight of meat)
- 4 teaspoons/12 grams caraway seeds (0.25% of weight of meat)
- 2 teaspoons/5 grams ground allspice (0.1% of weight of meat)
- 2 teaspoons/5 grams ground coriander (0.1% of weight of meat)
- 15 feet 42- to 55-millimeter hog casings, soaked in tepid water for at least 30 minutes

1. Grind the meat through a well-chilled ¼-inch (6-millimeter) grinder plate. Mix in the sea salt, curing salt, starter culture, black pepper, sugar, garlic, caraway seeds, allspice, and coriander and mix thoroughly, by hand or with an electric stand mixer with a paddle attachment at medium speed, until the meat becomes sticky and the spices are evenly distributed. Refrigerate the batter until you are ready to stuff.

2. Stuff the batter into the prepared casing and form into 1-foot links, leaving the links attached. Record the total weight of the sausage.

3. Place the sausages on your smoke sticks and hang them in your fermentation chamber. Bring the fermentation chamber up to between 70°F and 75°F (21°C and 24°C) with 80% to 90% humidity for 24 to 48 hours.

4. Place the links on a rack on a sheet pan in the refrigerator, uncovered, and let dry overnight.

5. Hang the sausages on a smoke stick in a cold smoker and cold smoke for at least 12 hours and up to 24 hours.

6. Hang the sausages on a smoke stick in a cool (55°F/12°C), dark environment with 75% humidity until the sausages have lost one-third of their original weight.

7. The dry-cured sausages are now ready to eat. You can store them in your refrigerator for up to 6 months.

LOP CHONG

Lop chong, often referred to as Chinese sausage, is a simple smoked and dry-cured sausage. As with with kielbasa in eastern Europe, there are lots of variations of lop chong from region to region in China. I've seen recipes that call for including duck meat, liver, pork blood, Sichuan pepper, Chinese five-spice powder, chile peppers, and on and on. Over the years I've played with different variations, but this simple recipe is always my starting point, and the one I come back to again and again. This smoky, sweet, and salty sausage is great in fried rice and stir-fries and keeps well in the fridge for a long time. If a little mold develops, don't worry; it's just a natural part of the process.

Makes approximately 20 5-ounce dry-cured sausages

- 10 pounds/4.5 kilograms pork shoulder, cubed and chilled (about 70% lean and 30% fat)
- ⅓ cup/113 grams fine sea salt or kosher salt (2.5% of weight of meat)
- Cure #2 or Veg Stable 504 (use supplier's recommended quantity for 10 pounds of meat)
- Starter culture (I use B-LC-007; use supplier's recommended quantity for 10 pounds of meat)
- 2 tablespoons/30 grams sugar (0.8% of weight of meat)
- 1½ tablespoons/15 grams minced garlic (0.3% of weight of meat)
- 4 teaspoons/10 grams ground cinnamon (0.2% of weight of meat)
- 1 tablespoon/10 grams ground black pepper (0.2% of weight of meat)
- ⅔ cup/150 grams soy sauce (3.3% of weight of meat)
- ⅓ cup/75 grams Chinese rice wine (1.7% of weight of meat)
- 15 feet 42- to 45-millimeter hog casings, soaked in tepid water for at least 30 minutes

1. Grind the meat through a well-chilled ¼-inch (6-millimeter) grinder plate. Mix in the sea salt, curing salt, starter culture, sugar, garlic, cinnamon, black pepper, soy sauce, and rice wine thoroughly, either by hand or using an electric stand mixer with a paddle attachment at medium speed, so that the meat becomes sticky and the spices are evenly distributed. Refrigerate the batter until you are ready to stuff.

2. Stuff the batter into the prepared casings and form into 1-foot links, leaving the links attached. Record the total weight of your sausages.

3. Place the sausages on your smoke sticks and hang them in your fermentation chamber. Bring the fermentation chamber up to between 70°F and 75°F (21°C and 24°C) with 80% to 90% humidity for 24 to 48 hours.

4. Place the links on a rack on a sheet pan in the refrigerator, uncovered, and let dry overnight.

5. Hang the sausages on a smoke stick and smoke in the cold smoker for at least 12 hours and up to 24 hours.

6. Hang the sausages in a cool (55°F/12°C), dark environment with 75% humidity until they have lost one-third of their original weight.

7. The dry-cured sausages are now ready to eat. You can store them in your refrigerator for up to 6 months.

DRY-CURED MEAT

Dry-cured meats are those that have been cured and air-dried in order to preserve them. As with smoking, the technique was originally used out of the necessity to preserve meat without refrigeration. Today it is associated with gourmet food items — think of *jamón Iberico* or Italian coppa. Most dry-cured meats are made from pork (the fat on pork is more stable than fat from other animals), but there are examples of beef (bresaola), goat or lamb proscuitto (*violino di capra*), and even dry-cured duck (duck prosciutto). Any cut of meat that you dry cure can be cold smoked as part of the process. Well-known examples of cold-smoked dry-cured meats include speck, country ham, some pancettas and dry-cured bacons, and *lonza* (pork loin). Like cold-smoked sausage, this is next-level stuff, and it requires a basic understanding of the dry-curing process and having a space where you can properly hang and dry cure. And, as is the case with bacon, this is a product where you can play a lot with flavor profiles.

Dry-cured meat is salted (cured) and air-dried in order to preserve it. Sometimes dry-cured meats, such as bacon, are also cold smoked to add a smoky flavor as well as to help preserve the meat.

SPECK

This recipe is for a very traditional speck featuring alpine flavors, but I have experimented a lot with different flavor profiles with fantastic results, including Korean spices, chile peppers and fennel, and garlic and honey. Once you've made a speck and properly wrapped it, it can last in your fridge for a very long time (months, or even a year). Remember that mold development — especially white, tan, and green mold — is just a natural part of the process. If a lot of mold starts to develop, or if you are uncomfortable with the mold development, just rub it off with a clean towel soaked with white vinegar or some wine. You can use speck like bacon or sausage, as a flavor base for a larger dish, but I like to slice it very thinly and serve it with good cheese, fresh bread, and some wine, beer, or hard cider.

Makes approximately 7 pounds

- 1 10-pound/4.5-kilogram boneless pork shoulder, skin on
- ½ cup/135 grams fine sea salt or kosher salt (3% of weight of meat)
- ½ cup/90 grams dark brown sugar, firmly packed (2% of weight of meat)
- Cure #2 or Veg Stable 504 (use supplier's recommended quantity for 10 pounds of meat)
- 4½ tablespoons/45 grams ground black pepper (1% of weight of meat)
- ¼ cup/45 grams ground allspice (1% of weight of meat)
- ¼ cup/45 grams ground juniper berries (1% of weight of meat)
- 1 tablespoon/10 grams ground bay leaves (0.2% of weight of meat)
- 1 teaspoon/3 grams mustard powder (0.06% of weight of meat)
- 1 teaspoon/3 grams ground nutmeg (0.06% of weight of meat)

1. Place the meat skin side down on a clean work surface. Remove any flaps of loose skin or meat. You want the meat to be as evenly shaped as possible; you can pound the meat with a pan or wooden mallet to help even it out. Record the weight of the pork.

2. To make the cure, combine the sea salt, brown sugar, curing salt, black pepper, allspice, juniper berries, bay leaves, mustard powder, and nutmeg in a bowl and mix thoroughly.

3. Completely and evenly cover the meat with the cure. Place the meat in a nonreactive container along with any extra cure that does not stick. Let cure in the fridge for 1 day for every kilo of meat, or 5 days total.

4. Wash the cure off the meat under cold water and vigorously rub it dry with a clean towel. Place the meat on a rack on a sheet pan and let rest, uncovered, in the refrigerator for a day or two until the surface has developed a good pellicle and is slightly tacky to the touch.

5. Roll and tie the meat, skin side out, so the shape is more or less even throughout. Cold smoke for 5 to 10 hours.

6. Hang in a cool (55°F/12°C), dark place with around 75% humidity until the meat has lost 30 percent of its original weight, about 6 months.

7. The speck is now ready to be eaten. To eat, thinly slice with a sharp knife. You can store it in the refrigerator for up to 12 months, wrapped with plastic wrap or vacuum packed.

COUNTRY HAM

In my opinion, country ham is the king of American curing traditions. Like barbecue, it tells us about the history of colonized America. Chefs like David Chang and Sean Brock have helped this particularly American dry-cured product reclaim its rightful place in our popular food canon and have helped to lionize country ham–producing families like the Bentons and the Newsomes. A ham requires patience but will pay off tenfold. Although this recipe calls for a ham (pork leg), I have also made it with a mutton leg, which was more common in colonial America. It can be sliced and served as is with bread, sharp mustard, and cheddar cheese. It can also be cooked and served alongside biscuits, eggs, and gravy, or it can be the main dish for the holidays.

Makes approximately 10 pounds

1¾ cups/560 grams fine sea salt or kosher salt (8% of weight of meat)

Cure #2 or Veg Stable 504 (use supplier's recommended quantity for 15 pounds of meat)

1 cup/140 grams dark brown sugar, firmly packed (2% of weight of meat)

7 tablespoons/70 grams ground black pepper (1% of weight of meat)

1 15-pound/7-kilogram fresh ham, skin on, aitch bone removed, trotter off

1. To make the cure, combine the sea salt, curing salt, brown sugar, and pepper in a bowl and mix thoroughly.

2. Place the ham on a clean work surface. Rub the cure all over the ham, being sure to get it into every nook and cranny. Give extra attention to the area where there is exposed bone. Place the ham and any excess cure in a nonreactive container just big enough to hold the ham. Place another nonreactive pan or a cutting board of some sort directly on the ham and weight it down using bricks or cinder blocks. Refrigerate for 3 days for every kilogram of meat, or 21 days total for a 15-pound ham.

3. Remove the ham from the cure and rinse under cold water. Vigorously rub it dry with a clean towel. Place the ham on a rack set on a sheet pan and let rest, uncovered, in the refrigerator for at least 12 hours and no more than 24 hours.

4. Cold smoke the ham for at least 18 hours and up to 48 hours.

5. Hang the ham in a cool (55°F/12°C), dark place with 75% humidity for 9 months to 2 years.

6. The ham is now ready to be eaten. To eat it, thinly slice with a sharp knife. You can store it in your refrigerator for up to 12 months, wrapped with plastic wrap or vacuum packed.

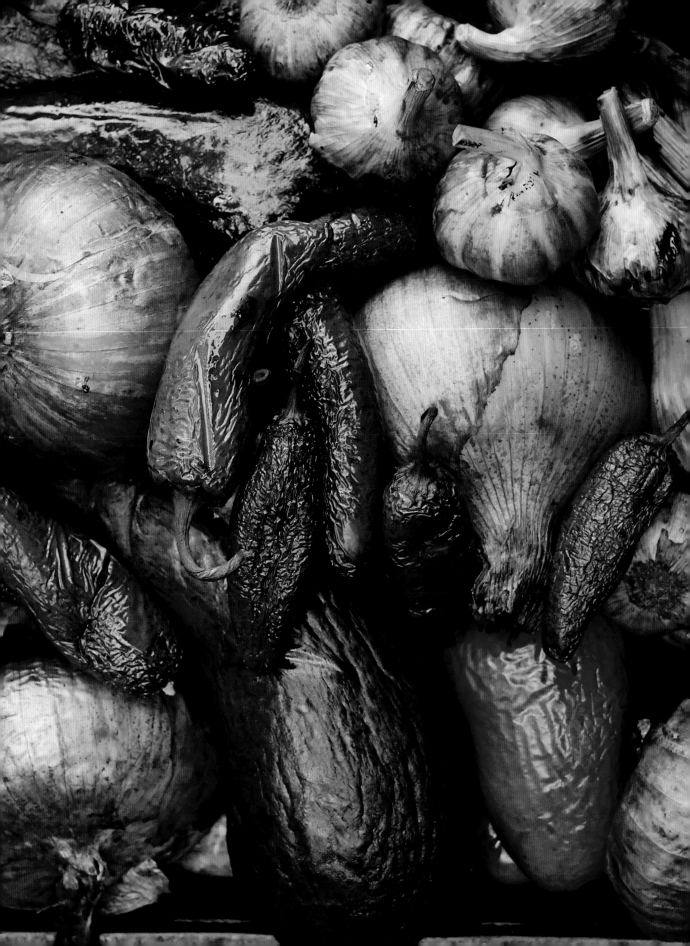

VEGETABLES, CHEESE, AND OTHER NONMEAT ITEMS

Cold smoking is a great way to add a smoky flavor to vegetables, hard cheeses, salt, and more. There are plenty of classic items to smoke, like chile peppers or cheddar cheese, but I have also enjoyed smoking garlic, sweet potatoes, and even honey. There are no real recipes or rules for this; it's all about exploration.

Generally speaking, you don't need a lot of smoke time for these items. Often I smoke them as an ancillary project to smoking something else, like a country ham or salmon.

For hard cheeses like cheddar or Gouda, 4 to 6 hours of cold smoking is enough to get that smoky flavor.

With liquids, like honey, maple syrup, and mustard, I pour them into a shallow roasting pan or sheet pan and stir occasionally during the smoking process to make sure they smoke evenly. These usually need only 3 to 5 hours.

I hang chile peppers from the roof of my smokehouse throughout the fall as I smoke other items, allowing them to dehydrate while also slowly developing smoky flavor.

I leave alliums (onions, shallots, garlic) whole and unpeeled and hang them in the cold smoker for 6 to 12 hours.

PART 4

BUILDING YOUR SMOKER

In part 2, I described the basic types of smokers and how to use them. In this section, I'll focus on how to build them, starting with the simplest and ending with the most complex. Some of these smokers are designed for only hot smoking or cold smoking, some involve hacking basic kitchen and outdoor equipment, and some involve building from the ground up. Some of the designs are permanent structures and some are temporary. The designs are meant to be simple and adaptable. It is important to have fun when you're building your smokers. Just as with choosing what fuel you are going to use, I encourage you to use whatever material you have available to you. As with everything in this book, my goal is to give you the basic framework for achieving your smoking goals, with the hope that from there you can expand, experiment, and adapt as needed.

A SHALLOW PIT FOR SMOKING ON A GRILL TABLE

Before you set up a grill table for smoking, you'll need to start with a pit. Lining the pit with stones will help retain heat for a longer cooking time. Remember to build your fire well before you plan on cooking to allow a nice bed of charcoal to build up. While you won't get the same intensity of smoke flavor as you would in an enclosed smoker, like a barrel smoker or kettle grill, this is a low-maintenance and versatile setup.

1. Find a site. When deciding where to locate your pit, consider the contours of the ground. It's ideal to build your pit into a berm, so there's shelter from the wind. If there are no suitable berms, try to locate the pit along a boulder or tree line that can help mitigate the wind. If the ground is completely level where you are and there are no physical barriers from wind, just dig a little deeper to create some protection from gusts.

2. Determine the size. You'll also need to consider how large you'd like your pit to be. What are you going to be cooking over the pit? Whatever the answer is, build the pit a little larger than that. In determining the dimensions of my pit, I thought about a roaster pig (around 100 pounds) or a goat and based my dimensions on that; consequently, our pit ended up being 5 feet by 3 feet. Once you've determined the right size for your needs, mark it on the ground.

3. Dig it. Dig the pit so that it's at least a few inches (but not more than 6 inches) below grade, including the depth of the stones you'll be using to line the pit. If you have heavy clay soil, consider laying down an inch or two of coarse builder's sand before laying the stones to improve drainage and reduce heaving from frost (if you live in a region where the ground freezes in the winter).

4. Lay the stone. To lay the stone, start at the center of the pit and move out from there. Place the stones evenly and relatively close together, but don't worry about making them perfectly tight. Once you've laid stone up to the edge of the pit, put down more sand to fill between the stones.

MAKE THIS YOUR FIRST SMOKER

Whether or not you plan on building any other kind of smoker, you should set up a stone-lined pit with a grill table. First, it won't take you longer than an afternoon to build. Second, it is the most useful, versatile outdoor cooking setup imaginable, and it will quickly become the center of all of your outdoor gatherings. Whether you want to smoke a rack of ribs, throw on some hot dogs and hamburgers, grill a whole striped bass, or cook up a ton of vegetables from the garden, it can all happen here.

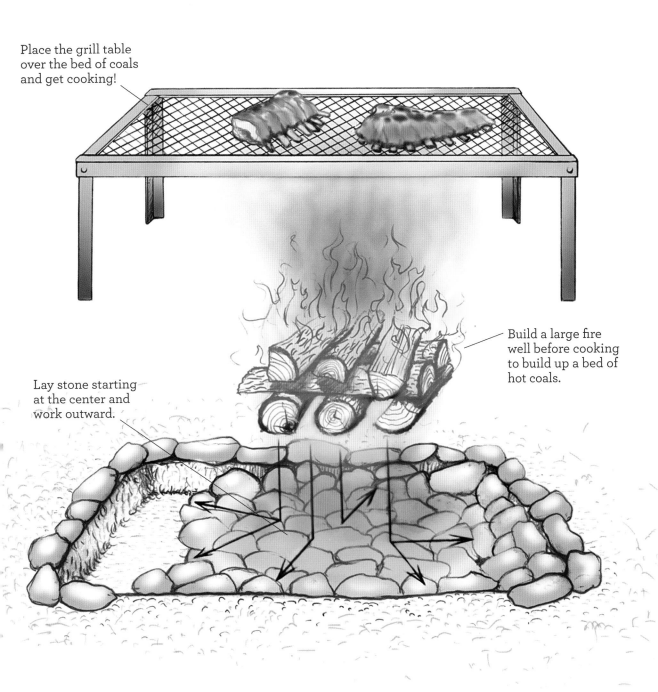

Place the grill table over the bed of coals and get cooking!

Build a large fire well before cooking to build up a bed of hot coals.

Lay stone starting at the center and work outward.

A DEEP PIT FOR IN-GROUND SMOKING

This style of pit is what is used in a lot of Mexican cooking, from the Yucatecan classic of *cochinita pibil* (little pig in a pit) to central Mexico's *barbacoa*. The main advantage of cooking in a pit in the ground is that the pit can hold heat for a long time and therefore cook for a much longer time, resulting in the supplest meat. It is also completely hands off once you have put the meat in the pit.

When building this kind of pit, you can keep it super–bare bones and literally just dig a pit in the ground, or you can get fancy laying stone or pouring concrete and laying firebrick. I would recommend starting simple; if this is a technique you love, then take it from there and build something a little more permanent. Likewise, when starting out, maybe try something a little smaller and less expensive than a whole pig or goat, like a brisket, a pork shoulder, or even just a whole head. This will allow you to get a sense of the charcoal depth needed, how to build the charcoal bed, and the timing of the cooking without putting too much pressure on yourself.

1. Choose a site. Pick a spot that will be relatively free of large roots and stones to make your digging experience easier. Keep in mind that what you will be left with is a bare patch of dirt, so you may want to locate it where it won't be in your direct view.

2. Determine the size. What are you going to be cooking in the pit? Whatever the answer is, build the pit a little larger than that. In determining the dimensions of my pit, I thought about a roaster pig (around 100 pounds) or a goat and based my dimensions on that. You want at least 6 inches of space between what is being cooked and the top of the pit. We built ours 4 feet long by 2.5 feet wide and 3 feet deep. In determining the depth of the hole, include the thickness of the material (stone or brick) you'll be laying in the base.

3. Dig the pit. Once you've determined the right dimensions for your needs, mark them in the earth and start digging. Be sure to keep some of the dirt dug from the pit available and nearby, as you will use it later.

4. Lay the stone. Once you've dug out the pit, you can start to lay down your stone or brick. As with the shallow pit (see page 156), if you have dense, clay soil, you might want lay down an inch or two of sand first. This will help with drainage and prevent heaving. Start to lay the stones at the center of the pit and spiral out from there; you want your stones to fit relatively closely together and evenly, but it doesn't have to be perfect. You can bring the stones or bricks as high up the walls of the pit as you would like, but the crucial part is the bottom of the pit. Some people like to build the stones or bricks up along the sides of the pit so that the walls can be used to support a grill within the pit.

5. Build a cover. In order to use the pit you will need a cover. You can use either a piece of sheet metal or a piece of plywood wrapped in aluminum foil or lined with thin sheet metal.

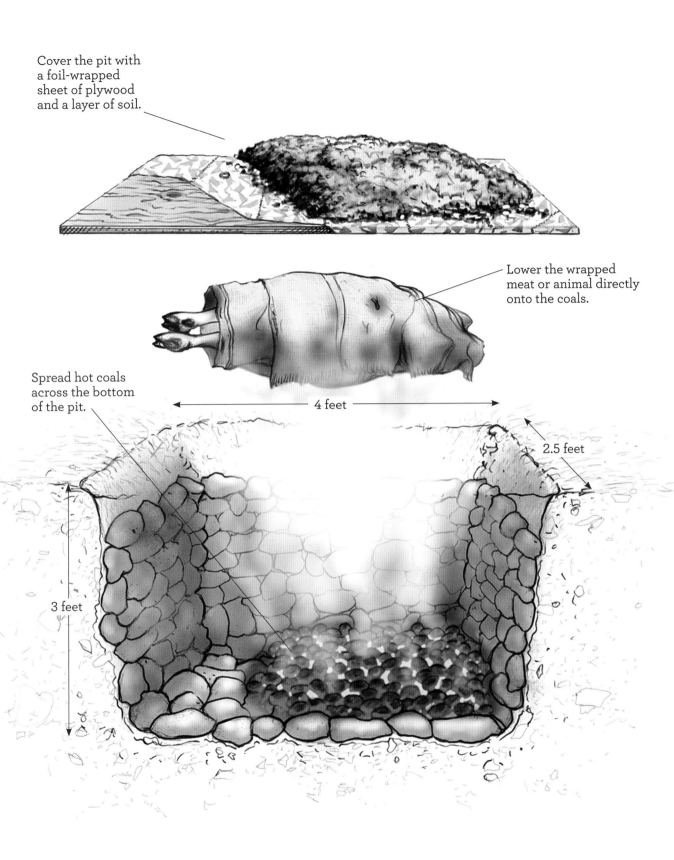

Cover the pit with a foil-wrapped sheet of plywood and a layer of soil.

Lower the wrapped meat or animal directly onto the coals.

Spread hot coals across the bottom of the pit.

4 feet

2.5 feet

3 feet

AN ABOVEGROUND PIT

This works on a similar principle to that of the in-ground pit. This is more like what you see in the American South or on the coast of western Africa. It is also nice because it is not a permanent structure. Once you are done using it, you can easily take away all of the building materials and either reuse them or rebuild your pit as needed. Over time, the plywood on the lid will burn away, but it can always be replaced.

MATERIALS

- Fifty-four 16×8×8-inch concrete blocks
- Three 40-inch lengths of rebar
- One 24×40-inch sheet of expanded metal (grill metal)
- One 4×8-foot sheet of thin metal
- One 4×8-foot sheet of plywood
- A box of ½-inch nails or screws

TOOLS

- Masonry chisel and hammer
- Hammer or drill

1. Choose a site. Choose a level spot that is away from buildings or anything else that could easily catch fire. Mark out an area that is 40 by 56 inches and clear the area of any flammable material. If the location you have picked has a lot of organic material that will burn (grass, roots, etc.), dig away the first couple of inches and backfill with sand or gravel.

2. Lay the first three courses of blocks. You will be laying five courses of blocks, each consisting of ten blocks. Lay the first course of blocks on the ground along the inside edges of the 40- by 56-inch space. When you lay the second and third courses, be sure to stagger the blocks. Staggering the blocks is an essential masonry technique employed to create a more stable structure. By staggering the courses of blocks, each course locks the one below it in place. Now remove one block from the first course on each of the short ends for airflow.

3. Place the rebar and grill. Once the third course is laid, place the three lengths of rebar evenly spaced (about 10 inches apart) across the pit. It helps to chisel out a notch in the blocks for the rebar to rest in; this eliminates any gap between the third and fourth layer of blocks. Lay the last two courses of blocks. Lay the expanded metal grill on the rebar.

4. Build the lid. Nail or screw the sheet metal to the plywood.

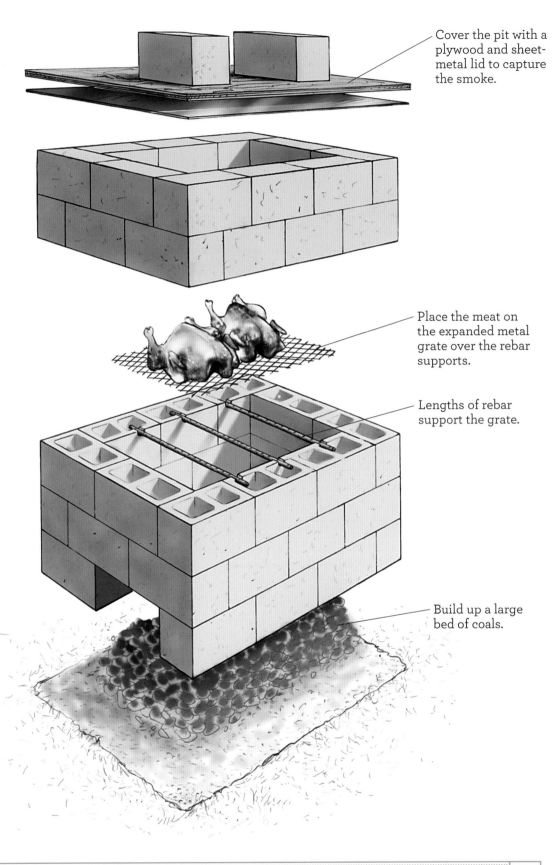

Cover the pit with a plywood and sheet-metal lid to capture the smoke.

Place the meat on the expanded metal grate over the rebar supports.

Lengths of rebar support the grate.

Build up a large bed of coals.

A HOT-SMOKE DRUM SMOKER

This design smokes meat much like your charcoal grill does; it's essentially a taller version of your grill, with more space for large quantities of meat, as well as large cuts. It's perfect for smoking bacon, multiple racks of ribs, whole birds, briskets, and pork shoulders, as well as tenderloins, small roasts, and chops and steaks. Like your charcoal grill, this smoker is only suited for hot smoking. If you really like this style of smoker but a 55-gallon drum isn't big enough, consider using an old oil tank. Large, offset smoker rigs are often made of these.

MATERIALS

- 55-gallon steel drum with lid
- Eight 1½-inch-long ¼-inch-diameter 20 TPI bolts with lock washers and nuts
- Two 22½-inch-diameter grill grates (a 55-gallon drum has a diameter of 23 inches and you want a grate that will fit within that)
- Standard gate pull handle with appropriate fasteners
- A can of high-heat engine paint

TOOLS

- Power drill with step bit
- Propane blowtorch
- Respirator

Vent holes

Meat thermometer

Bolts support the grates.

Air intake holes

1. Source your drum. The safest and easiest way to start is to buy a new 55-gallon drum. When you buy a new drum, you know that it hasn't been used for anything toxic, and you can choose one that doesn't have a liner. (Some drums have chemical liners that are extremely difficult to remove, requiring burning at high heat and a metal grinder to grind them away.) The only thing inside a new drum will be a coating of rust inhibitor that can be burned out easily with a propane torch at the same time you remove the original exterior paint. If you do decide to use an old and/or found drum, make sure you know what was stored in it. If you are unsure of whether or not the drum has a liner, assume it does and go through the burning-off process just to be on the safe side.

2. Burn off the paint. For this step, it's best to wear a respirator, as burning off the paint will release a lot of chemicals and particulate matter. Light your blowtorch and slowly move it in a sweeping motion across the surface of the drum. Both the original paint and the interior rust inhibitor will come right off with the high heat. Alternatively, you can build a fire inside the drum; it should burn to at least 1,000°F/538°C (this is a good time to use an infrared thermometer gun). It's best to keep the fire burning for a couple of hours. Use a blowtorch to burn the paint off the lid of the drum, being careful not to apply too much heat in one location, as the thin lid might warp. Use a clean rag to wipe off the drum and lid completely to remove any excess paint and dirt.

3. Drill holes for the grates. Measure 7 inches down from the top of the drum and drill four holes, equally spaced around the drum (about 18 inches apart). The holes should be large enough to allow the ¼-inch-diameter bolts to fit through, but not so large that the head of the bolts will slip through. This is where you'll eventually place the cooking grate.

Measure 12 inches up from the bottom of the drum and drill four more holes, equally spaced around the drum (about 18 inches apart). Again, the holes should be large enough to allow the ¼-inch-diameter bolts to fit through, but not so large that the head of the bolts will slip through.

This is where you will place the grate that will hold the charcoal and woodchips.

Install the bolts so that they stick out into the barrel.

4. Drill holes for air intake and venting. Measure 3 inches up from the bottom of the drum and drill three ¾-inch holes equally spaced around the drum, about 24 inches apart. These will be your air intake holes.

On the lid, drill eight ¾-inch holes 3 inches in from the edge of the lid and equally spaced, about 6½ inches apart. These will act as your air/smoke vents.

5. Drill holes for the handle and thermometer. Depending on the type of handle you'll be attaching to the lid, drill the appropriate holes for that. (I used a standard gate pull handle for mine.) You should also drill a hole in which you can put your thermometer. I use a dual probe thermometer, so I drilled two small holes in the lid, just large enough to get the probes through.

6. Paint the drum (optional). If you want to make sure your smoker lasts a long time and doesn't rust, you should paint it with a high-heat engine paint that has been rated upwards of 500°F/260°C. First be sure to remove any leftover steel shavings from drilling that might have fallen into the drum. From inside the drum, use painter's tape to cover the holes you just drilled; this prevents spray paint from getting inside the drum or the inside the lid. Securely place the lid back on the drum. Paint the entire exterior of the drum, including the bottom of the drum and the top of the lid. Allow the paint to dry completely.

7. Install the charcoal grate. Once the paint has dried, insert the 1½-inch bolts and tighten them with the lock washers and nuts into the two sets of four holes you have drilled around the top and bottom of the drum. Insert one of the grill grates so that it rests on the bottom set of bolts. This will hold the charcoal and woodchips.

8. Attach the handle. Secure the handle to the lid, using the hardware that comes with the handle.

A COLD-SMOKE DRUM SMOKER

Cold smoking is an easier process to manage than hot smoking because you don't have to worry about maintaining a consistent temperature; in fact, you don't want heat from the fire to enter the chamber (hence the name cold smoking). Once you have a good burn going and are producing a nice, steady stream of smoke, it requires very little attention. You'll need to check on the fire now and then and occasionally restock it with wood.

Building a cold smoker is a little more complicated than building a hot smoker, however, because you have to create two chambers: one that holds the food and smoke, and one that holds the fire that generates the smoke. The two chambers must be connected to each other so the smoke can travel from one to the other while losing the heat of the fire.

This model starts out the same way the hot-smoke drum smoker does. In order to maintain a low-enough temperature in the smoke chamber, though, you have to use a separate chamber to contain the fire — a firebox connected to the smoke chamber with a stovepipe. This smoker is great for making cold-smoked bacon, fish, sausage, and smaller pieces of cured meat.

As with the previous design, these instructions call for using a 55-gallon drum, but any number of other objects will also work (see page 73). You just have to be sure that the object is food safe, that it can be vented to exhaust the smoke, and that there's some way to hold the meat in it. For a firebox, I've seen people use old garbage cans, kegs, large pots, terra-cotta planters, cast-iron wood burning stoves, or simply a hole in the ground. The main thing is to make sure that whatever you're using as a firebox can hold a fire safely, and that the fire can continue to burn in it over a long period time. One creative and simple solution I have seen and like a lot is connecting two grills together with piping: one grill serves as the firebox and the other as the smoke chamber.

MATERIALS

- 55-gallon steel drum
- Standard gate pull handle with appropriate hardware
- A woodstove, steel drum, metal trash can, terra-cotta planter, or large cast-iron kettle to serve as the firebox (alternatively, you can dig a pit)
- One 22½-inch-diameter grill grate
- Four 1½-inch-long ¼-inch-diameter 20 TPI bolts with lock washers and nuts
- At least 4 feet of 6-inch-diameter stove piping
- Two 6-inch-diameter stovepipe elbows
- Paint (optional)

TOOLS

- Power drill with step bit
- Reciprocating saw with blade for cutting metal
- Propane blowtorch
- Metal file or metal grinder

The smoke chamber should stay below 90°F/32°C.

The stovepipe allows smoke to travel from the firebox to the smoke chamber.

The firebox is set below grade.

2.5 feet

1. **Acquire and prepare your drum.** Follow the instructions on page 163 for removing paint and rust inhibitor. Feel free to paint the drum. High-temperature paint is not necessary, as your drum will never reach a high heat in cold smoking.

2. **Drill holes for the cooking grate.** Measure 7 inches down from the top of the drum and drill four holes equally spaced around the drum, about 18 inches apart. The holes should be drilled large enough to allow the ¼-inch-diameter bolts to fit through, but not so large that the head of the bolts will slip through. This is where you will eventually place the cooking grate. Install the bolts so that they stick out into the barrel.

3. **Saw a hole for the stovepipe.** Flip the drum over so that the closed end is up. In the center of the bottom end, mark a 6-inch-diameter circle. Drill a hole within the 6-inch circle, large enough to allow your reciprocating saw blade through it. Using the reciprocating saw, cut out the 6-inch circle. This is where you will feed the stovepipe

in. Make sure you can easily slide the stovepipe into the newly cut hole. If not, file or grind the edge of the hole until you can.

4. **Drill holes for venting and the handle.** Measure 3 inches in from the edge of the lid and drill eight equally spaced ¾-inch holes, about 6½ inches apart. Drill holes as needed and install the handle on the lid.

5. **Choose a spot for your smoker, preferably where the grade is on an incline.** Decide where you're going to install your cold-smoke drum. If you want this to be a permanent installation, you can bury some of the features, like the stove-pipe and the firebox, in the ground. The stove pipe should rise slightly as it goes from the fire-box to the smoking chamber. Having a pitch on the stovepipe ensures that the smoke is pulled into the chamber from the firebox. Mark on the ground where you'll put the smoking chamber, the firebox, and the pipe. There should be at least a 4-foot distance between the firebox and the smoking chamber.

Option 1: The Buried Firebox

1. **Dig a trench for the stovepipe.** The trench should be wide enough to fit the 6-inch stove-pipe and should keep a 5- to 10-degree pitch going upward from the firebox to the smoking chamber. A good rule is that the trench should rise 1 inch for every foot, creating a 5-degree angle, so that over a 4-foot run, the pipe will be 4 inches higher on the smoke chamber end than at the firebox end.

2. **Dig a pit to use as the firebox.** Your firebox — the space where you burn the fuel to generate smoke — can be nothing more than a hole in the ground. If you do just dig a pit, make it about 2 feet deep and 18 inches in diameter. If you'd rather have a firebox that doesn't flood or erode, you can use another steel drum, a metal gar-bage can, a cast-iron kettle, a large terra-cotta planter, or (one my favorite solutions) a small wood-burning stove. Whatever you use for the

firebox, you'll need to be able to connect the stovepipe to it, and it should be enclosed or you must be able to cover it so that the smoke is forced into the stovepipe and up into the smok-ing chamber. A piece of scrap metal or a large flat stone works well as a lid.

3. **Lay the pipe.** Lay the stovepipe so that it enters the firebox and reaches where you intend to place the smoking chamber. Attach the stove-pipe elbows, with one elbow facing downward into the firebox and the other turned upward to where the 55-gallon drum smoking cham-ber will be. Carefully place the drum over the upward-reaching stovepipe, fitting the end of the stovepipe into the hole you previously cut out of the bottom of the drum.

4. **Install the grate.** Install the grill grate by plac-ing it on the four bolts.

Option 2: Aboveground Installation

If you want this to be an impermanent installation, don't feel like digging, or don't have a place in your backyard with a suitable incline, you can install all this aboveground. The basic principles of installing it in the ground still apply; the pipe should rise 1 inch for every foot, creating a 5-degree angle, so that over a 4-foot run, the pipe will be 4 inches higher on the smoke chamber end than at the firebox end. This design requires lifting the smoking chamber on cinder blocks to achieve the proper stovepipe angle.

1. Choose a firebox. A small cast-iron woodstove works well for this. These are relatively easy to find, inexpensive, designed to hold fires that burn for a long period of time, and built to have the smoke piped out of them. Alternatively, you could use another steel drum, an old metal garbage can, or anything that can hold a fire. Just remember that you'll need to connect the stovepipe to the firebox, and that you'll need to be able to cover the fire (if the firebox is open), forcing the smoke to travel into the stovepipe and up to the smoking chamber.

2. Connect the stovepipe. Fit the stovepipe to the firebox, using one of the stovepipe elbows. The pipe needs to rise 1 inch for every foot of length. If you are using 4 feet of stovepipe, your pipe should be 4 inches higher on the smoke chamber end than on the firebox end.

3. Raise the smoking chamber. Calculate the height of the smoking chamber end of the stovepipe based on the required pitch. This is the height at which the bottom of the smoking chamber should sit.

Prop up the smoking chamber to the necessary height. I use cinder blocks because they're inexpensive and I always have them around. You could build a wood frame or weld a metal one, if you felt like it.

4. Connect the smoking chamber. Connect the smoking chamber to the firepit with the pipe.

5. Install the grate. Install the grill grate by placing it on the four bolts.

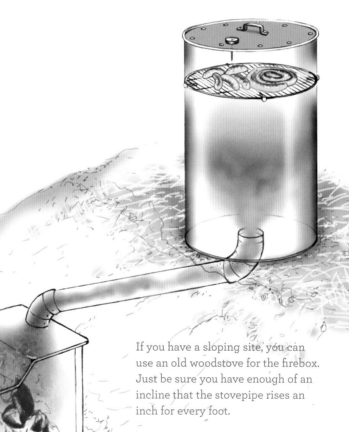

If you have a sloping site, you can use an old woodstove for the firebox. Just be sure you have enough of an incline that the stovepipe rises an inch for every foot.

THE TRI-PURPOSE SMOKEHOUSE

When choosing a spot for your smokehouse, make sure the location is not near any buildings or objects that could easily catch fire. Ideally, find a place where there is a slight pitch in the ground level, so that the firebox can be situated at a lower level than the smoke chamber. This ensures that the stovepipe will have an upward pitch from the firebox to the smoke chamber, with less digging on your part. Having a pitch on the stovepipe ensures that the smoke is pulled into the chamber from the firebox.

This is a building project that requires familiarity with construction and masonry principles and techniques. In building my smokehouse I was extremely fortunate that my brother Will is a professional builder who has a lot of experience with natural and traditional building techniques, including building with cob. Although smokehouses are traditionally made from brick, stone, or now concrete blocks, cob made the most sense for us. Cob is just another masonry technique, like building with adobe, stone, brick, or concrete blocks. We had the skills, we could use a lot of the material from digging out the foundation for the cob, and it's fun to build with.

If you don't know how to build with cob, or don't feel like learning, you can follow the same basic design and use other masonry materials. Adobe, brick, concrete blocks, and stone are all great materials for building smokehouses and work perfectly for this basic design.

Finished dimensions: 5 × 5 × 10½ feet tall

MATERIALS

- 6-inch-diameter stovepipe (at least 5½ feet long)
- One 6-inch-diameter stovepipe elbow
- 6-inch-diameter stovepipe cap
- 4 cubic yards of gravel
- Thirty-seven 80-pound bags of concrete mix
- 50-pound tub of high-temperature mortar
- Two sheets of ¾-inch CDX plywood
- Four 8-foot 2×2s
- One (1-pound) box of 2-inch decking screws
- One 48-inch length and one 12-inch length of 2-inch iron pipe
- Two 2-inch iron pipe elbows
- 298 firebricks (each 4½×9×2½ inches)
- A pallet of wall-building fieldstone for the foundation
- 3 cubic yards of cob, made up of 3 cubic yards of soil (in our case we used the soil from the excavation of the foundation, which had a good combination of clay, sand, and silt) and 3 bales of straw (for more explanation of cob composition and construction, see page 174)
- Twenty-four 6-inch 2×4s (for anchors)
- Two (1-pound) boxes of 3-inch 16-penny nails
- Doorframe: two 6-foot 2×6s, two 4-foot 2×6s
- Door stops: one 8-foot-long 1×4
- Vent: two 13-inch 2×6s, two 6-inch 2×6s
- Insect screen: 8 inches × 12 inches
- Ridge beam: one 7-foot 2×6
- Rafters: ten 6-foot 2×6s
- Top plates: two 5-foot 2×6s
- Blocking for fly rafters: twelve 1-foot 2×6s
- Purlins: eight 1-inch × 3-inch × 8-foot boards
- Three 10×3-foot metal roofing panels
- One (1-pound) box of ½-inch self-tapping metal screws

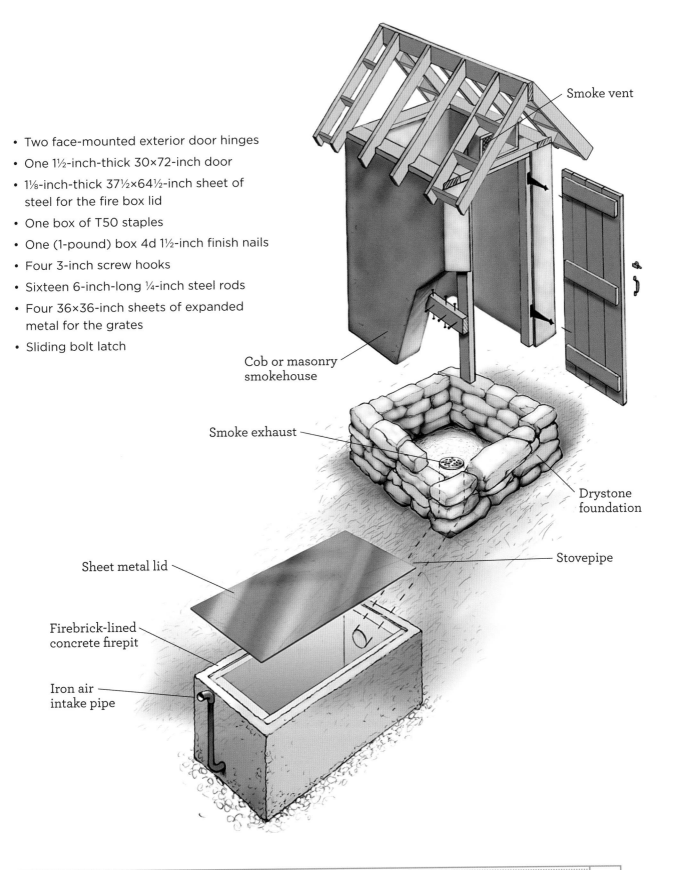

- Two face-mounted exterior door hinges
- One 1½-inch-thick 30×72-inch door
- 1⅛-inch-thick 37½×64½-inch sheet of steel for the fire box lid
- One box of T50 staples
- One (1-pound) box 4d 1½-inch finish nails
- Four 3-inch screw hooks
- Sixteen 6-inch-long ¼-inch steel rods
- Four 36×36-inch sheets of expanded metal for the grates
- Sliding bolt latch

Smoke vent

Cob or masonry smokehouse

Smoke exhaust

Drystone foundation

Stovepipe

Sheet metal lid

Firebrick-lined concrete firepit

Iron air intake pipe

DIGGING THE FOUNDATIONS

1. Mark out and dig the foundation of the smokehouse. Using spray paint or chalk, mark the location of the 5-foot by 5-foot smokehouse base. Dig a pit for the foundation that goes below the frost line. Here in western Massachusetts, that's 4 feet deep. In southern Arizona, there is no frost line. If you have no frost line to worry about, just dig till you hit solid ground free of plant roots.

2. Mark out and dig the firepit. Using spray paint or chalk, mark a 37½- by 64½-inch area where you will locate the firepit. Ideally, you want one of the short ends of the firepit to be 48 inches from the center of where the smokehouse will be. Dig the pit 46½ inches deep.

3. Dig a trench for the stovepipe. The trench should be wide enough to accommodate the 6-inch-diameter stovepipe and long enough to connect the smokehouse to the firepit. The trench should be dug at a pitch that declines from the smokehouse to the firepit by 1 inch for every horizontal foot (keep the dirt on hand for backfilling). Once the pipe is laid, the top of the elbow should be at grade level, and the firebox

end of the stovepipe should extend about 3 inches into the pit.

4. Install the smoke exhaust end into the smokehouse floor. On the smokehouse end of the stovepipe, attach an 18-inch section of stovepipe to the elbow extending upward, using the self-tapping metal screws, as plumb as you can get it. The final floor height will be 18 inches above grade.

At the end of that pipe, install a baffle. The baffle helps diffuse the smoke so that it fills the chamber evenly. For our baffle, we bought a 6-inch stovepipe cap and drilled about twenty ⅛-inch holes into it.

5. Backfill with gravel. Backfill the foundation of the smokehouse with some of the gravel so that it is 2 inches below grade and level. Be careful to keep the stovepipe plumb.

THE FIREPIT

6. Backfill the pit and pour the concrete floor. Backfill the firepit with a 6-inch layer of gravel. Mix and pour a 3-inch-thick slab of concrete over the gravel to form the floor of the firepit; you'll need seven bags of the concrete mix. Allow the concrete to set completely.

7. Build a form for the foundation walls. Using ¾-inch plywood and decking screws, build a box without a top or bottom that is 37½ inches tall, 31½ inches wide, and 58½ inches long. To construct the box, cut two pieces of plywood for the two long sides to 58½ inches long by 37½ inches wide. Then for your short sides cut another two pieces of plywood to 30 inches long by 37½ inches wide. The sides of the box will be held together by 2×2 cleats. Cut four pieces of 2×2 into 37½-inch lengths for your cleats. Using the decking screws, screw the 2×2s to the inside corners of the box (be sure to screw through the 2×2 into the plywood), making sure the box comes together to be 37½ × 31½ × 58½ inches. Cut four 30-inch lengths of 2×2 and place them evenly apart across the inside width of the box to keep the plywood from bowing in under the pressure of the wet concrete. Center the frame in the hole.

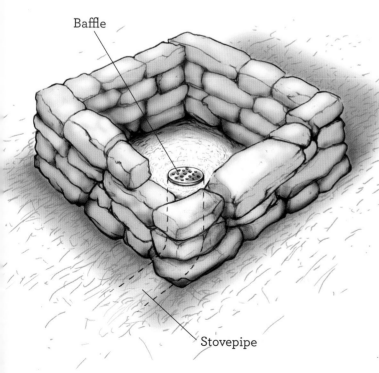

Baffle

Stovepipe

8. Place the pipes. On the short ends, you'll need to place the smoke-exhaust stovepipe and the iron air-intake pipe, then pour around them. To make the air-intake pipe, use a 48-inch length of 2-inch-diameter iron pipe, with elbows attached to each end, facing out in opposite directions. Place one end of the pipe 5½ inches above the floor of the pit with the elbow facing into the pit, level with the interior edge of where the 3-inch-thick concrete wall will be. Add the 12-inch length of pipe to this end, extending into the pit. This pipe will draw air into the pit, feeding the fire for smoking, and will direct the airflow in the proper direction, so the smoke flows through the stovepipe and into the smokehouse.

9. Pour concrete for the sides. Once the slab for the floor of the pit is set you can pour the concrete sides. Mix the remaining concrete.

Pour 3-inch-thick concrete walls on the two long sides of the pit.

For the wall closest to the smokehouse, where the stovepipe leads in, pour a 3-inch-thick concrete wall around the stovepipe, fixing the stovepipe in the concrete wall. On the opposite wall, place the air-intake pipe (you will need to dig out a little more dirt on this end to make room for the pipe) and pour a 3-inch-thick concrete wall,

fixing the air-intake pipe in place, making sure the pipe remains plumb. Once the concrete has set, remove the form by unscrewing the cleats.

10. Measure the pit. At this point, the pit should have an interior space that is 37½ inches deep, 31½ inches wide, and 58½ inches long. These dimensions are important because they fit the firebrick dimensions perfectly.

11. Line the pit with firebrick. Lay firebrick on the concrete slab floor and along the four walls. We dry-laid the bricks for the floor and used high-temperature mortar for the bricks going up the walls. Apply a ⅛-inch layer of mortar to each brick as you build up. Do not cover the intake or exhaust pipes with brick.

Once the firebrick is laid, you'll have a final interior dimension of 35 inches deep, 22½ inches wide, and 49½ inches long: perfect for roasting a whole animal.

12. Make a lid for the pit. For the lid, we had a friend fabricate one out of ⅛-inch-thick steel in three sections (to make it more manageable to lift). You can use a piece of plywood with thin sheet metal attached to it, but from experience, I can tell you that it will burn out over the course of a long burn.

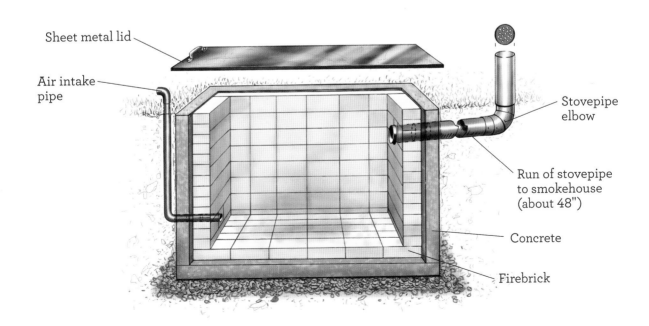

Sheet metal lid

Air intake pipe

Stovepipe elbow

Run of stovepipe to smokehouse (about 48")

Concrete

Firebrick

13. Lay the foundation stone. Find the largest, flattest stone from your pallet of fieldstone and set it aside. On top of the gravel foundation for the smokehouse, lay a dry-stack stone stem wall, 18 inches high and at least 12 inches wide. A stem wall is a supporting structure that is used to join the base of a building to the walls. On your last course, lay the large flat stone you had set aside to serve as the threshold of your door.

The stone wall protects the cob from ground moisture, splash back from rain, and snowfall. If you're building your smokehouse with concrete block, brick, or stone, you won't need to lay a separate stone foundation — you will just start laying the block, brick, or stone for the house directly on the gravel bed.

14. Backfill with gravel. Backfill the stem wall with the remainder of your gravel up to the height of the stovepipe. This is your smokehouse floor.

15. Mark out the door opening for the smokehouse on your stone threshold. This should be the width of your door (we used a salvaged door 30 inches wide × 72 inches tall) plus 3 inches for a 2×6 doorframe, so we marked out a door space that was 33 inches wide.

16. Build the cob walls. Start to build up your cob walls on top of your stem wall. The general rule of thumb for cob walls is that they should start at a thickness that is at least 10 percent of the height of the wall; with a 6-foot-tall wall, that would be

TRIAL AND ERROR: BUILDING AN EFFICIENT FIREPIT

We ultimately made our pit as we describe here after trying other, simpler firepits. First we used an old woodstove, but we found it was inconvenient to have to feed the fire so often during a long cold smoke. On top of that, the pit itself (where the stove was dug into the ground) flooded frequently.

The concrete- and firebrick-lined pit we ended up building is material and labor heavy, but we fill it just once every 12 hours or so, and it doesn't flood. It also solved the problem of how to supply enough air to the fire — one of the biggest hurdles we dealt with in working out the design for Frazier.

If you choose to build a simple pit for your smoker (as described in the designs on pages 158 and 166) rather than pouring concrete and laying firebrick, you'll need to find a way to provide airflow. For example, if you dig a traditional earthen firepit, you'll need to prop open the lid, very slightly, on the end farthest from the smokehouse, so that air can feed the fire and create airflow that pushes the smoke into the stovepipe and up into the smokehouse.

7 inches thick. We built ours 9 inches wide at the base and tapered to 6 to 7 inches at the top.

17. Make anchors and set them in the cob. To make the anchors, take the 6-inch 2×4s and hammer a few 16-penny nails into one of the narrow sides of them so the nails are sticking out halfway. The nails give the cob something to grab onto, securing the wood anchors into the cob wall. Build up a few inches of cob and set anchors into the walls, nail side into the cob, on both sides of the door opening. Use a level to make sure the end of each 2×4 anchor is plumb with the door opening. As you build up the cob walls, place these anchors every 24 inches. For a 72-inch-tall door you will need four anchors on each side of the door opening. Later you will be attaching a wood doorframe to the ends of these anchors.

18. Set anchors for the racks. As you build the cob walls, install wood anchors in the cob every 12 inches as you build up to support the racks of the smokehouse. Use the same principle used for the doorframe anchors of hammering nails sticking halfway into one side of wood, giving something for the cob to grab onto, securing the wood into the cob walls. The lowest rack should be 2 feet above the floor. On the two walls adjacent to the door, set four anchors into the cob: two on either wall, spaced 24 inches apart and level with each other.

19. Build the doorframe. Continue to build up the walls with cob until you reach the height of where the top of the door will be.

Using 2×6s, build a doorframe based on the measurement of your door. The doorframe consists of two vertical pieces of 2×6s and a header. The header is made up of two 2×6s doubled up on the flat that extend 4 inches past the verticals on each side.

Using the decking screws, screw the 2×6 vertical frame members into the anchors; shim where necessary. Attach the first piece of the header to the top of the vertical 2×6 doorframe members. Attach the second identical piece directly on top of this.

At this point the tops of the cob walls and top of the doorframe header should be at the same height. Install a top plate on the two walls perpendicular to the door. These should be 2×6s with nails sticking out of the bottom (using the same technique as with the anchors) to grab the cob. They should extend 2 inches inside of the corners of the building and be parallel to each other. Install these while the last couple inches of cob are still somewhat wet.

20. Make and install a vent. A vent is important for proper airflow and smoke movement. Build the frame for the vent with an interior dimension of 6×10 inches out of 2×6s. Staple the insect

MIXING AND WORKING WITH COB

Cob is a mixture of clay-rich soil, sand, straw, and water. It's just one of many ways to use soil as the base of a building material. The word "cob" comes from England (it originally referred to the rounded lump of soil mix you make when you're building), where they have been using this form of building material for thousands of years. Other regions of the world may use a slightly different composition for similar purposes, like adobe in Mexico.

Start by making a test batch. For the test batch, use one 5-gallon bucket of sand and one 5-gallon bucket of clay soil. Mix them together on a tarp on the ground. Once they are completely mixed, slowly add one-quarter of a 5-gallon bucket of water. It's always better to add water a little bit at a time; it's much harder to make a mix drier than it is to make it wetter. An effective method for mixing is to stomp the mixture with your bare feet. Roll the tarp with the mixture on it, like you're rolling a burrito. Then unroll the tarp; if the mixture is wet enough, it will stick together in a solid mass. If it needs more water, the mixture will be crumbly. You know the mixture is too wet if you can't make a softball-size ball and drop it from shoulder height without it turning into a pancake. It should flatten out a little but still hold together.

Make a test brick. Once you've created a mixture with the right consistency, make a potato-size test brick and let it dry in the sun for a day. The next day, if it has stayed together, doesn't have big cracks (or a lot of small cracks), and feels sturdy — you shouldn't be able to crush it with your hand — you have a good mixture. If it has a lot of cracks, add more sand to your mix. If it crumbles under the pressure of your hands, increase the amount of clay soil. If that doesn't work, your soil doesn't have enough clay in it

and you should find different soil or try adding manure. One way to tell if your soil has enough clay is to add some water to it and try to roll a snake; if it breaks apart easily, you don't have enough clay in your soil.

Add straw to the mix. Once you feel confident in your mix, add a couple of big fistfuls of straw. To mix in the straw, flatten out the mixture on the tarp and spread the straw evenly around. Stomp it in until it is well incorporated in the mix. Do another burrito roll with the tarp and stomp it again. Add a few more handfuls of straw and repeat the process. Do one final burrito roll and unroll the tarp, leaving the mixture in a roll. Try to pull off a big chunk from the roll of cob. You'll know you've added enough straw if it's difficult to pull the chunk away from the roll.

Start building. Now you're ready to start building with the cob. You only want to mix up enough cob for one day of building. For your initial layer of cob, start with a slightly wetter mix and smear it onto the surface you are building up from — in this case, the top of your stem wall. Then build up the cob wall by taking chunks of cob and pressing them down into the previous layer, using your thumbs or a similar-size stick to push it down. Build up equally around all sides. Try to keep the thickness of the wall consistent. As you build, check your walls for plumb every hour. If your walls are bulging, cut off the excess with a hand saw. If they are tapering in, fill out the hollows by working in a wetter mix of cob. Always keep the tops of your walls protected from drying out too much or getting rained on with a tarp. When starting out for the day, always begin with a wetter mix.

Thanks to Will Levin for supplying this information.

screen to one side of the frame; this will be the side that faces outward. Center the vent over the doorway on the header and attach the vent to the top of the header.

21. Build up the gable ends. The wall with the door and the one directly opposite it need to be built up with cob to carry the ridge beam of the roof. Build up the cob in the form of a triangle with a 3-foot peak to support the ridge beam.

The roof pitch should be about 45 degrees, so, for a 5-foot-wide smokehouse, the bottom of the ridge beam should be about 2½ feet above the top of the top plates.

22. Install a 2×6 ridge beam into the peak of the cob wall. Using the same principle previously applied to the anchors, attach 16-penny nails sticking halfway out to the ends of the 2×6 that will be in contact with the cob. Once the cob in which the anchors have been installed is set, install the ridge beam. The ridge beam should extend 1 foot past the walls on either end to ensure that the gable ends are well protected.

23. Attach the rafters and plywood. Continue building the roof, employing standard gable roof construction. Cut the rafters to 5 feet with a 45-degree plumb cut. The plumb cut end of the rafters will be attached to the sides of the ridge beam. To lay out your bird's-mouth cut for the rafters, temporarily screw one rafter to the ridge beam and to the end of the top plate. Hold a carpenter's pencil on the top plate and scribe the top plate to the rafter. Cut out the piece you scribed. Use this rafter as a template to mark the bird's-mouth cut on five of the other rafters, and make the bird's-mouth cut on them. Nail the rafters to the ridge beam and top plates. Two sets should be flush with the gable end walls; the other set should be centered between the gable end walls. Using the 16-penny nails, nail the three pieces of blocking perpendicularly to each gable end rafter, spaced equally apart. Nail fly rafters to the blocking and ridge beam. Perpendicular to the rafters, nail purlins to the rafters, 15 inches on center.

24. Install roofing material. We recommend finishing with a screw-down metal roof, but you could also use wood shingles or shakes. Will used our smokehouse roof as a chance to improve his shake-making skills, so we are graced with a white oak shake roof, which also helps with venting.

25. Install racks. For racks in the smokehouse we used expanded sheet metal resting on ¼-inch steel rod pegs set in the wood anchors. We also installed hooks on the ridge beam to hang larger cuts of meat, chiles, and other food items.

26. Hang the door. Screw face-mounted hinges 6 inches from the top and bottom of the door. With the hinges mounted on the door, hold the door in place in the doorframe. Screw the hinges to the edge of the doorframe. Mount whatever latching system you prefer; we used a sliding bolt latch.

27. Install door stops. Mark a line all along the doorframe 1½ inches inset from the outside of the doorframe. Cut the 1×4 into three 1×1s. Cut one length to the inside dimension of the header. Using finish nails, nail it to the inside of the line you just marked; this is your header stop. Measure from the threshold to the header stop you just installed. Cut the remaining two 1×1s to that measurement and, using finish nails, nail these to the inside of the line on the vertical of doorframe. These are your side stops.

VARIATION: A SMOKEHOUSE BUILT WITH CONCRETE BLOCKS

If building with cob feels like too much work or is too unfamiliar, you could build the smokehouse with concrete blocks. Because concrete blocks come in a standard size of 8 × 8 × 16 inches, the completed smokehouse will be 4 feet by 4 feet, rather than 5 feet by 5 feet. Using blocks also eliminates the need to build an initial stem wall and reduces the labor time by a fair amount; you can build straight from the ground up.

Another benefit is that you can drill, screw, and anchor directly into the blocks using a masonry bit. This is helpful for installing metal pegs to hold the smoking racks and securing the doorframe to the blocks using masonry screws.

For this variation, you will need 81 8 × 8 × 16-inch concrete blocks, three bags of mortar, and 1 cubic yard of sand.

Dig out a foundation, as on page 170.

Lay the blocks using mortar, making sure to stagger them on each course.

The top of the doorframe should measure 6 feet and be level with the other three concrete block walls.

Use masonry screws to attach the 4-foot-long 2×6 top plates to the top of the doorframe and the top of the other three walls.

Screw the vent, centered, above the door.

On top of the vent, nail one 18½-inch 2×6 centered on the vent and perpendicular to it. Nail a 24½-inch 2×6 to the top plate to the opposite wall, also centered. These will hold the ridge beam.

Nail the ridge beam to the studs.

Because the concrete block smokehouse is a foot smaller on each side than the cob smokehouse, we need to adjust the size of the roofing panels by 1 foot each. Other than that, proceed as described on page 175.

We recommend siding the gable ends of the walls with 1×8 shiplap pine, but you can cut a piece of plywood to close in the gable ends instead.

RESOURCES

WEBSITES FOR SMOKING TECHNIQUES, ADVICE, AND RECIPES

AmazingRibs.com
http://amazingribs.com

Meats and Sausages
www.meatsandsausages.com

SUPPLIES, EQUIPMENT, AND INGREDIENTS

Butcher & Packer Supply Co.
248-583-1250
www.butcherpacker.com

Craft Butchers' Pantry
www.butcherspantry.com

Penzeys Spices
800-741-7787
www.penzeys.com

BIBLIOGRAPHY

Boetticher, Taylor, and Toponia Miller. *In the Charcuterie: The Fatted Calf's Guide to Making Sausage, Salumi, Pâtés, Roasts, Confits, and Other Meaty Goods.* Ten Speed Press, 2013.

Byres, Tim. *Smoke: New Firewood Cooking.* Rizzoli International Publications, 2013.

Cairo, Elias, and Meredith Erickson. *Olympia Provisions.* Ten Speed Press, 2015.

Carroll, Joe, and Nick Fauchald. *Feeding the Fire: Recipes and Strategies for Better Barbecue and Grilling.* Artisan, 2015.

The Culinary Institute of America and John Kowalski. *The Art of Charcuterie.* John Wiley and Sons, 2011.

Danforth, Adam. *Butchering Poultry, Rabbit, Lamb, Goat, and Pork: The Comprehensive Photographic Guide to Humane Slaughtering and Butchering.* Storey Publishing, 2014.

Dunlop, Fuchsia. *Land of Plenty: A Treasury of Authentic Sichuan Cooking.* W. W. Norton and Company, 2001.

Epstein, Ed. *Build a Smokehouse.* Storey Publishing, 1981.

Fearnley-Whittingstall, Hugh. *The River Cottage Meat Book.* Ten Speed Press, 2007.

Franklin, Aaron, et al. *Franklin Barbecue: A Meat Smoking Manifesto.* Ten Speed Press, 2015.

Husbands, Andy, and Chris Hart. *Pitmaster: Recipes, Techniques and Barbecue Wisdom.* Fair Winds Press, 2017.

Lamb, Steven. *The River Cottage Curing and Smoking Handbook.* Bloomsbury Publishing, 2014.

Mallmann, Francis with Peter Kaminsky. *Seven Fires: Grilling the Argentine Way.* Artisan, 2009.

Marcoux, Paula. *Cooking with Fire: From Roasting on a Spit to Baking in a Tannur, Rediscovered Techniques and Recipes That Capture the Flavors of Wood-Fired Cooking.* Storey Publishing, 2014.

Mariansky, Stanley, and Robert Marianski. *Meat Smoking and Smokehouse Design,* 3rd ed. Bookmagic, 2012.

McGee, Harold. *On Food and Cooking: The Science and Lore of the Kitchen.* Scribner, 2004.

Raichlen, Steven. *Project Smoke*. Workman Publishing, 2016.

Reavis, Charles, and Evelyn Battaglia, with Mary Reilly. *Home Sausage Making, 4th Edition*. Storey Publishing, 2017.

Ricker, Andy, and JJ Goode. *Pok Pok: Food and Stories from the Streets, Homes, and Roadside Restaurants of Thailand*. Ten Speed Press, 2013.

Ruhlman, Michael, and Brian Polcyn. *Charcuterie: The Craft of Salting, Smoking, and Curing*. W. W. Norton and Company, 2005.

———. *Salumi: The Craft of Italian Dry Curing*. W. W. Norton and Company, 2012.

Thiam, Pierre, and Jennifer Sit. *Senegal: Modern Senegalese Recipes from the Source to the Bowl*. Lake Isle Press, 2015.

Weiss, Jeffery. *Charcutería: The Soul of Spain*. Agate Surrey Books, 2014.

Yoskowitz, Jeffery, and Liz Alpern. *The Gefilte Manifesto: New Recipes for Old World Jewish Foods*. Flatiron Books, 2016.

METRIC CONVERSION CHARTS

Unless you have finely calibrated measuring equipment, conversions between U.S. and metric measurements will be somewhat inexact. It's important to convert the measurements for all of the ingredients in a recipe to maintain the same proportions as the original.

WEIGHT

US	METRIC		TO CONVERT	TO	MULTIPLY
0.035 ounce	1 gram		ounces	grams	ounces by 28.35
¼ ounce	7 grams		pounds	grams	pounds by 453.5
½ ounce	14 grams		pounds	kilograms	pounds by 0.45
1 ounce	28 grams				
1¼ ounces	35 grams				
1½ ounces	40 grams				
1¾ ounces	50 grams				
2½ ounces	70 grams				
3½ ounces	100 grams				
4 ounces	112 grams				
5 ounces	140 grams				
8 ounces	228 grams				
8¾ ounces	250 grams				
10 ounces	280 grams				
15 ounces	425 grams				
16 ounces (1 pound)	454 grams				

VOLUME

TO CONVERT	TO	MULTIPLY
teaspoons	milliliters	teaspoons by 4.93
tablespoons	milliliters	tablespoons by 14.79
fluid ounces	milliliters	fluid ounces by 29.57
cups	milliliters	cups by 236.59
cups	liters	cups by 0.24
pints	milliliters	pints by 473.18
pints	liters	pints by 0.473
quarts	milliliters	quarts by 946.36
quarts	liters	quarts by 0.946
gallons	liters	gallons by 3.785

US	METRIC
1 teaspoon	5 milliliters
1 tablespoon	15 milliliters
¼ cup	60 milliliters
½ cup	120 milliliters
1 cup	240 milliliters
1¼ cups	300 milliliters
1½ cups	355 milliliters
2 cups	480 milliliters
2½ cups	600 milliliters
3 cups	710 milliliters
4 cups (1 quart)	0.95 liter
4 quarts (1 gallon)	3.8 liters

TEMPERATURE

TO CONVERT	TO	
Fahrenheit	Celsius	subtract 32 from Fahrenheit temperature, multiply by 5, then divide by 9

COMMON OVEN TEMPERATURES

US	METRIC
200°F	90°C
225°F	110°C
250°F	120°C
275°F	140°C
300°F	150°C
325°F	160°C
350°F	180°C
375°F	190°C
400°F	200°C
425°F	220°C
450°F	230°C
475°F	250°C
500°F	260°C
550°F	290°C (broiling)

ACKNOWLEDGMENTS

First and foremost, I need to thank and acknowledge my brother Will Levin. Without him this book would not exist. I would never have been able to design our smokehouse without him. And if he hadn't built it, and troubleshot it, and rebuilt various elements of it, I would not have such an amazing smokehouse with which to hone my smoking skills and to write a book about. He was also an indispensable and incredibly patient resource for writing the building instructions. And always ready, willing, and able to eat whatever food I put in front of him.

Thanks to my wife, Silka Glanzman, who was so supportive and patient throughout this process. When I was in my most anxious and unbearable moods, she was there for me and able to calm me down. Thanks also to the rest of my family, my parents, Tom Levin and Susan Engel, my brother Sam Levin, and my sister in-law Nicole Campanale, who were always willing to give me recipe feedback, read things over, and be sounding boards for me.

Thanks to the wonderful colleagues and partners in crime I have had over the years: Jack Peele, Jamie Paxton, Jazu Stine, and Jordan Archey (I only work with people whose name starts with J). It is with them that I was able to bounce around ideas, explore new techniques and recipes, and in general learn, play, and grow. Working with them has made me a better butcher, meat smoker, and cook. Thanks also to my mentor, Bryan Mayer, who not only taught me the craft of whole animal butchery but helped me realize that the ethics and values behind our craft are inseparable from it.

Thanks to the dedicated farms and farmers I have worked with over the years and who have helped provide the meat for my recipe testing and for the photo shoots: Sean Stanton and Tess Diamond of North Plain Farm, Colby and Schuyler Gail of Climbing Tree Farm, Georgia and Lee Rainey and Anna Hodson of Kinderhook Farm, Ashley Amsden and Michael Gallagher of Square Roots Farm, and Jerry Peele of Herondale Farm.

This book would not be in your hands if it weren't for the guidance of my amazing editor, Carleen Madigan. I am in awe of how she was able to sculpt the manuscript I handed her into what it is today. I am also grateful to art director Jeff Stiefel, who was able to turn my words into a beautiful visual experience. And, of course, thanks to Joe Keller, whose superb eye and gorgeous photography elevate this book to another level.

INDEX

KEEP YOUR CREATIVITY COOKING WITH MORE BOOKS FROM STOREY

BY PAULA MARCOUX

Rediscover timeless techniques and exciting new ones — from roasting on a spit to baking in a masonry oven — with this comprehensive guide to all the tools, instructions, and recipes you'll need to master wood-fired cooking.

BY ANDREA CHESMAN

Reintroduce flavor and texture to your home cooking with this definitive reference for processing and preserving animal fats. In addition, 100 recipes highlight favorite traditional dishes like matzoh ball soup, pork tamales, New England baked beans, jelly doughnuts, and so much more.

BY CHARLES G. REAVIS AND EVELYN BATTAGLIA, WITH MARY REILLY

Detailed directions for popular charcuterie techniques such as dry curing and smoking — plus 100 mouthwatering recipes ranging from breakfast sausage to global favorites like mortadella, liverwurst, chorizo, kielbasa, and more — make this the most comprehensive sausage-making reference available.